Nightmare Nation

Redefining the Pursuit of the American Dream

Jessie C. Conners

Protégé Press

For further information, please contact:
info@nightmarenation.com

Book designed by:
Arbor Books
19 Spear Road, Suite 301
Ramsey, NJ 07446
www.arborbooks.com

Printed in the United States of America

Nightmare Nation: Redefining the Pursuit of the American Dream
Jessie C. Conners

1. Title 2. Author 3. Personal Finance/Investing

Library of Congress Control Number: 2007922833

ISBN-10: 9793259-0-0
ISBN-13: 978-0-9793259-0-8

Dedicated to Mom and Dad
Through the happy, sad and crazy times
I love you so much

TABLE OF CONTENTS

Introduction

Wealth and Want: Don't Burn the Furniture to Heat the House

Donald Trump said the "F" word to me. On national TV. In front of twenty million people.

"You're fired!"

Just like that, I was off season one of *The Apprentice*. I was also utterly devastated.

For a few days. Until I realized that I'm not defined by anyone's opinions, especially an opinion based on choppy editing and measured by television ratings.

After that experience, I went back to my successful start-up businesses and went on to become much more successful than I ever could have been as anyone's apprentice. So thanks, Donald. You actually did me a favor.

What I did get from *The Apprentice* was a little more knowledge about the way the world works, and, because I've always believed that knowledge is power, I soon realized that I didn't need to follow in someone else's footsteps to be successful. I'd create wealth using my own experiences, ingenuity and opportunities of my own making—just as I'd been doing all my life.

During childhood, I sold chicken eggs and gathered porcupine quills in hopes that every penny that jingled into my piggy bank would someday make me wealthy. Sounds like one of your grandfather's stories? Well, I'm only 24 years old.

Through hard work and careful investing, I turned those early dreams of wealth into *my* reality and in a short time went from nothing to something a lot more substantial.

I may be young but I've already got a lot to say about the pursuit of financial freedom and I understand that changing your perspective about money helps you see the difference between material wealth and *actual* wealth—it also helps you realize and reach your true goals in life.

Fame may only last fifteen minutes, but my eyes have been pried open irreversibly. Following my appearance on the show, I've spoken in over seventy different cities from coast to coast. Every week, I travel to a new area and stay at a different hotel, yet I somehow see the same people. Well, not literally the same...but they're in the same situation. I'm talking about Americans who are living off borrowed money and borrowed time in a desperate attempt to sustain a lifestyle that doesn't make them any happier. Americans are drowning in their own debt. They're putting temporary wants in place of true wealth. Rising interest rates, job insecurity, lost pensions and a shaky housing market are just a few of the factors creating a potential disaster for the average American. Consider this statistic: In 1980, there were 1.27 personal bankruptcy claims per 1,000 Americans. By 2004, it had increased to 5.32 out of every 1,000; that's a rise in personal bankruptcy of 320%. Then in 2005, right before tougher bankruptcy laws were passed making it harder to wipe out personal debts, filings went up another 30%, reaching an all-time record high of 2.1 million bankrupt Americans. This is a trend you can't afford to be a part of.

The latest statistics since February 2006 show that the number of bankruptcies is rising again, with 79% of those filing citing medical bills and job loss as the major causes. Obviously, a lot of Americans are being caught financially unprepared without any savings in the bank to fall back on.

Young Americans (25–44) are the second-highest demographic filing for bankruptcy, spending 24% of their income on debt pay-ments—that's a quarter out of every dollar they earn that they're just giving away each month to credit card companies. Just think about that. Remember the shock and horror when you got your first paycheck and almost 25% of it was given straight to the government in the form of taxes? Nowadays, young people are willingly handing over the same amount to credit card companies (and Uncle Sam *still* gets his piece of the pie)! That kind of debt ensures starting out your adult life at a tremendous disadvantage.

But by coming to my seminars, people are finally trying to find a way out of the vicious cycle of spending and borrowing that has led to their overleveraged, precarious financial position.

Our parents and grandparents have experienced large corporate layoffs, been affected by bursting economic bubbles, seen their pension plans evaporate and let their short-term wants dictate their lives. They are now wondering how they will afford to retire or, in many cases, if they will retire.

This book is for the 75 million people out there in their 20s to 40s who witnessed the financial instability that beset previous generations and are determined not to let themselves get sucked into the same black hole. It is for people who are ready to redefine wealth in their lives and, by doing so, *redefine their lives*.

———————

I didn't have a TV when I was a kid but I know that for most people of my generation, ever since you saw a Cabbage Patch commercial, money has been ingrained in your head as being plentiful and "stuff" is the primary symbol of status. I say "money," you hear "Manolo." Our generation has grown up in a world where wealth is defined by your handbag or the jeans you wear. But what happens when you have your own family who is dependent on you for basic needs? Will you still satisfy all of your wants with a little piece of plastic that has a nasty habit of charging 20% interest rates? How long will it take before you see yourself going down the same path as previous generations?

I may still be young, but I've weighed the opinions of others who have more experience and knowledge than I do and I've worked hard all my life to create my own wealth. Nothing has ever been handed to me and maybe that makes me appreciate it that much more. I grew up with no running water or electricity, lived in an orphanage in Mexico and didn't get a college education. But these experiences have given me a unique perspective of wealth from both sides—a perspective that has helped me earn financial freedom at lightning speed.

Before you go out to test drive that new BMW, I want to caution you that this book is not some get-rich-quick scheme; rather, it's a get-rich-smart guide to changing your entire perspective on wealth, finding your true passion and obtaining and maintaining economic independence. It will help you get started today on crafting a game plan for your future so you don't have to worry about how you'll dodge the pitfalls that come with financial insecurity. I mean, between airbrushed models and plastic surgery ads, don't we all have enough insecurities as it is?

I may be just twenty-something, but my unique life experiences, which include both amazing successes and my share of failures, have helped me craft a strategy for success in seven steps that will make you think twice about your time, your money, your future and what you really want out of life. You can get all the things you want without losing sight of what really matters.

And doesn't that "trump" all?

CHAPTER ONE

SAVE YOURSELF

Why You Need This Book

Let me start off this chapter with a startling statistic: If something doesn't change—and soon—close to 13% of hardworking Americans will retire below the poverty line *(www.npr.org)*. That means that more than one in every ten people who just read that sentence will die poor. Do you want to take that chance?

Imagine it. You work hard all your life, support your family and then just when you should be able to start relaxing and stop working, you have nothing to show for all your years of effort. The scary thing is, you may not have to imagine it at all—that's the all-too-real situation facing millions of Americans. And I don't mean in some distant future for our grandchildren to deal with. This is already happening here and now in 2007.

If you think about it, the signs are already here. Social security is drying up, Medicare isn't covering personal costs, and the prices for daily expenses that we used to take for granted (like pharmaceuticals, education costs, rent and trans-portation) are becoming astronomical and almost unmanageable for the average American. You know that kind, diligent, 75-year-old greeter at Wal-Mart? Someday that may be your spouse, your mother, or you.

This chart *(from www.randomuselessinfo/gas price.com),* showing the average price of gas over almost three decades, illustrates a disturbing trend in the recent cost of living. With fuel prices way higher than they were only four years ago, at around $3 a gallon, what do you think will happen in the near future? Did you spend more on gas than last year—and did these extra cents a gallon add up to higher monthly credit card bills? Even if the price of gas goes back down, rest assured

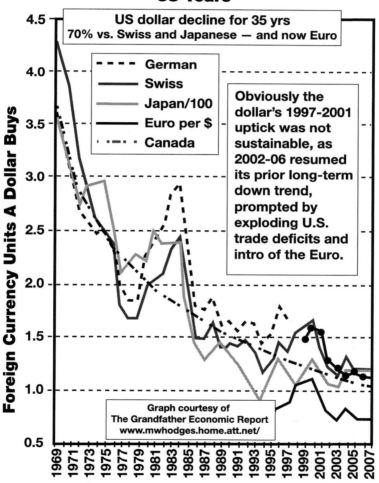

Dollar Foreign Exchange Loss
38 Years

US dollar decline for 35 yrs
70% vs. Swiss and Japanese — and now Euro

- ▪ ▪ ▪ ▪ **German**
- ▬▬▬ **Swiss**
- ▬▬▬ **Japan/100**
- ▬▬▬ **Euro per $**
- ▪ ▪▪ ▪ **Canada**

Obviously the dollar's 1997-2001 uptick was not sustainable, as 2002-06 resumed its prior long-term down trend, prompted by exploding U.S. trade deficits and intro of the Euro.

Foreign Currency Units A Dollar Buys

Graph courtesy of
The Grandfather Economic Report
www.mwhodges.home.att.net/

something else will go up: the cost of heating, road tolls, postage stamps. The Federal Energy Regulation Commission has already warned that "customers may experience rate shock" when they open their energy bills next year (that's when state regulations currently controlling utility prices expire).

Ask yourself: Do you have even more debt than this time last year? How will you be able to get by in the not-so-distant future if you can barely do it now? The answer: You won't. Unless you make a change. Now.

I'm not trying to freak you out (well, a little...but for your own good). What I'm trying to do is help you *figure it out*. With 55% of American families reporting credit card debt—a figure that has more than doubled in the past decade—it's obvious that the mishandling of personal finances has become a national epidemic and that learning how to handle your money should become an immediate priority.

Right now, the U.S. federal debt is around $8.2 trillion. No, that's not a typo. Trillion. That number seems almost unfathomable, right? Until you consider that the total debt of ordinary Americans (including mortgages, loans and outstanding credit card balances) is $11 trillion dollars. We, as citizens, owe more than our entire government. So it's not only politicians who can't balance the budget!

A recent issue of *Newsweek* reported that for the first time in our recorded history, our national savings rate has gone negative. More women filed for bankruptcy last year than graduated from college…you've come a long way, baby, but you're headed in the wrong direction! People are borrowing against their future earnings to pay for their extravagant lifestyles today. How can they do this? Too easily. Families are averaging about seven credit cards apiece and credit card companies are making it easier than ever for us to get them. Why? Because they know that we charge more than we can pay. They lower their credit standards, increase the interest rates to compensate, then watch the profits roll in.

The example the magazine cites is this: If a family owes $9,000 and their credit card has an 18% interest rate, even if they pay the 2% minimum on the balance each month, it will take 47 years—and close to $33,000—to pay off that original debt. The stuff they bought doesn't seem so worth it now.

But even with soaring prices and a sluggish economy, the typical American family still overspends and ignores the warning signs, racking up an

average of $9,000 of debt on their credit cards—
while the credit card companies, unfazed by the
country's financial slump, continue to show yearly
profits of more than $30 billion. In other words, the
money you should be saving is being spent to make
these companies rich. So why not start thinking
about your future and make yourself rich instead?

As this chart shows (*http://mwhodges.att.net*),
American citizens' habit of spending more than
they save is not only dangerous for the individual, but for the entire country. It has caused the
dollar value to drop against German, Swiss,
Japanese and Canadian currency as well as the
Euro. If you've been to Europe lately, you know
how expensive everything seems because of the
exchange rate.

On top of that, our government has been
running giant deficits, so it borrows from foreign
countries in order to make up the financial
difference. According to *The New Yorker*, more
than $3 trillion has been invested in the U.S.
from foreign governments buying our debt.
China has bought over $321 billion of U.S.
Treasuries and Japan $640 billion. Even Saudi
Arabia and Russia, who have not been our
closest allies, own big stakes in America. We
don't even own our own money anymore! And if

those foreign governments stop buying U.S. Treasuries, the dollar will drop even further. The American government is setting a bad example for its citizens by borrowing more than it's able to pay back and relying on others to keep it afloat.

While all this economic information may seem arcane and distant from your everyday life, I put it in here for a good reason. A lot of Americans don't realize why they are paying so much for gas or why there seem to be fewer well-paying jobs in the twenty-first century. The causes are macroeconomic and geopolitical in nature—and the more you know, the better you can prepare. With oil prices, terrorism, a soft real estate market, and jobs being shipped overseas, it seems like only a matter of time before another Great Depression. But in every economic depression or slump, there are individuals who are able to prosper. They're the ones who recognize the issue in advance and act accordingly, rather than ignoring it and carrying on spending recklessly.

Think you have to be a financial genius or come from a rich family to be successful today, given everything that's going on in the world? You don't. I'm proof. My family was so financially stressed that we eventually sold everything we owned. About a decade later, I had worked my way to achieving financial security. The difference came down to changing my perspective about money—it was a matter of being lost then having *saved.*

The End of the World As I Knew It

I came to understand what debt was all about at a very young age. I was 11 years old. It was almost winter. It was approximately 3 a.m. when I woke up from the freezing cold, and, as my head emerged from the thick denim quilt, I could actually see my breath in front of me. I had forgotten to stoke the stove and all the windows were iced over in the tiny mobile home that my family now lived in.

It wasn't always like this. Just a few months ago, my parents and three siblings were in a beautiful house in the suburbs of St. Paul, Minnesota. Then, suddenly, that world came to an end when my parents decided to move us out of our comfortable reality.

We sold everything we had—furniture, clothes, my toys, which were more like companions to me than possessions—and now here we were, in the middle of Nowhere, Wisconsin, with no electricity, no running water, no Christmas, no more birthday parties and no more tears to waste.

I stopped myself from crying and got up to tend the stove.

From this experience, I learned just how devastating many little choices could add up to be and how my version of financial stability could disappear in such a short amount of time. We had lost our home just as if it was carried away by a tornado, and it tore us apart as a family and as individuals—that's the kind of heart-wrenching impact that debt and creating the illusion of financial security can have on people's lives. And I know it all too well.

The American Dream Turned Nightmare

Some of my earliest memories in life were of our showpiece home in one of the most prestigious suburbs of St. Paul. When I think back, I some-times wonder if I'm remembering it correctly—if the sun really did shine so brightly in our sprawling backyard that I can feel it on my face even now. I'm not just picturing it through a lens of nostalgia. It really was that perfect. What I didn't realize was that my family was living the American Fantasy—not the American Dream.

My father had been the youngest-ever graduate of the Northwestern Chiropractic College. He achieved that milestone at the same age I am now—24. Once my father received his doctorate, he settled comfortably into a thriving chiropractic practice and my family settled down in an upper-middle-class lifestyle, which would prove to be short-lived.

With that upscale standard of living comes the unspoken expectation to stay on par with the neighbors. Actually, I believe our parents' genera-tion encourages keeping up with the Joneses. My mother began to obsess about perfection and presentation—things to please other people—and, like many thousands of others before and since, my parents began to live beyond their means.

In a short period of time, our American Dream life came crashing down around us. It was right after our family trip to Hawaii when I knew something in my 8-year-old reality had gone desperately wrong. Worry and stress filled our household and I had no idea why or how to make it go away.

Since my parents' temporary economic success didn't bring with it the long-lasting happiness that they—and so many others—presumed it would, they turned away from the world in disgust and looked toward the spiritual. Not as a new beginning but as an end.

My father was given a book that outlined a specific date for the second coming of Jesus Christ. From this and the Book of Revelations (the last book of the Bible), my parents took verses out of context and interpreted them in a literal way, which to us kids was frightening. They told us about the rapture, when Jesus was going to come out of the sky and call all true Christians into Heaven while the world as we know it literally comes to an end.

I was pulled out of school immediately and told that the world would be coming to an end on October 8th—only ten months away—at exactly 11:55 a.m. My parents didn't waste any time informing everyone else about the significance of this date and the bloodbath that would ensue if they didn't repent. The same went for us kids, too. We were to immediately "get our lives in order." From that point on, my sister and I were no longer schooled, were not allowed to watch television, had limited play time and were severely ordered to dedicate what was left of our young lives to God. It was strict and it was serious—it was the apocalypse in fourth grade.

We had left our house a few days before October the 8th and drove up to Canada. With the last of the money that we had left after my father quit his job ten months earlier, we rented a house on the lake. It had a little swing out back and it was the perfect place to watch the sky and wait for Jesus.

The morning of October 8th was freezing cold and I woke up in terror. I remember distinctly that, over our last breakfast, my sister spilled orange juice on my favorite doll. Normally, I would've been upset but that day I didn't even care because all I could think of was how I'd never see that doll again since my life, and everyone else's, was almost over.

My family and I bundled up in our snowsuits that morning to stay warm while we waited. Then there was the toughest part…saying goodbye. We hugged, we kissed, we cried. I looked at my little brother's cute 4-year-old cheeks puffed up around his confused eyes and, not knowing what would happen when we were taken to Heaven, I bit the inside of my own cheek to stop myself from crying in front of him. I'm even tearing up now as I write this.

Needless to say, the world didn't end and we were left with no choice but to start over from nothing. We drove back to our home. The whole fourteen-hour drive seemed to be in silence. Some people may think we would have been cheering from joy after the realization that our lives weren't over but it was just the opposite. In fact, my life was over. Everything that I believed in, everything that I thought was true, the heroes that I put my trust in, my faith, my whole life...it was all gone.

Nine-year-old me was sitting in our old suburban van as it drove through the Canadian countryside. Peering out the window, I realized, as crazy as it seems to one so young, that the only thing I really knew and could honestly believe in was the distance from my head to my toes and to the extension through my fingertips. I could only really believe in me.

As we returned to the doorstep of the home we thought we'd never return to, I carried my duffel bag down to the room I thought I'd never sleep in again, and I was certain no one else would ever again have the luxury of controlling my ideas because I had lost faith in everything but myself. All I knew for a fact at that moment were my actions and my feelings. And my dreams? Well, I wasn't going to let anyone take those away from me again.

This is when we moved to the middle of Nowhere, Wisconsin. That day really was the end of the world for me and from then on I dreamed of financial independence as a way to make my life more secure.

And I eventually found that security by myself, with no bitterness at all toward my parents. Like so many of us today, they were young and naïve. I love them to pieces—and who knows where I would be if I hadn't gone through those formative times? Let's face it, many kids would be *so* much better off without TV and their video games!

Don't Charge Your Life Away—Take Charge of Your Life!

Too many people make the same mistake my parents made. No, I'm not talking about selling everything and preparing for the apocalypse...that one's a little unique. I mean confusing "looking" successful with "being" successful. Image starts to take on a life of its own—a very expensive life that they can't actually afford. I've come to think of it as a "lease on life"—buying into an image of success which doesn't really belong to you.

There's an old assumption that acting successful is the first step to becoming successful, when in fact it's a step toward financial failure. A young man goes out and leases a car he can't afford in order to impress clients or coworkers. Or a young woman charges expensive clothing that makes her look like a million bucks but puts her thousands of dollars into debt. Not smart. And, after all, success comes from smart choices.

Examples like these are what I call "dumb debt"—going in debt over unnecessary items that may give you the image of success but will never give you the satisfaction of success and will actually lead you further away from your goals. Dumb debt is very much the opposite of "intelligent investing."

Americans are now experiencing the highest level of debt since the Great Depression. Yet unlike that era when economic struggle and a scarcity of belongings were in evidence, debt today has its roots in the exact opposite reason—mass consumption and a preponderance of possessions. We spend over our heads, we live above our means and we don't get any closer to where we want to be. In fact, this cycle of spending puts the idea of economic independence further out of reach. It doesn't make our lives any better and, when the shopping high wears off and you're left only with unpaid bills and a bunch of stuff that you didn't need, you'll see just how shallow and short-term that way of life was.

Face the Future

Society today places too much emphasis on instant gratification. You know that pair of designer jeans you can't live without? Trust me, you can live without them. Put the plastic away and practice a little self-restraint. It'll pay off in the future. But those jeans? They'll be out of fashion by the time you finish paying them off.

For a lot of people—especially young adults who are just starting out on their own—the idea of saving for the future is a foreign one. They can't imagine someday having to support their own families, pay off a mortgage or save for retirement. For many members of our generation, the concept of "long-term planning" loosely translates into "What are you doing next weekend?"

There are plenty of reasons for this:

A) We aren't really taught about finances in school (which is something that *needs* to change) other than remembering to bring our lunch money—and, if you forgot, well…you could always mooch off your friends.

B) Our parents were too overwhelmed with their own financial situations to explain it all to us and they often shoulder the burden of saving for our futures while the money we earn from part-time jobs is used for immediate purchases such as entertainment, gas or clothing. Unfortunately, this arrangement reinforces the idea that cash is disposable and paychecks are meant to be spent in as short a time as humanly possible—a concept that follows us into adulthood.

C) In our society, money is the last taboo. We talk *about* sex, plastic surgery, politics and religion as openly as if we were on Oprah's couch. But we talk *around* money.

D) Credit card companies target younger demographics with their "buy it now, pay it off later" philosophy that only pays off for them.

E) We live in uncertain times when the future doesn't only feel like it's a long time away—it sometimes seems like a long shot altogether.

With war, terrorism, epidemics and natural disasters in the news daily, a good percentage of my age group has adopted a "live for today" attitude instead of saving for an unknown future that may not come. However, every generation has had to contend with issues like these—world wars, atomic bombs and stock market crashes—yet tomorrow did come and, hopefully, they weren't caught unprepared.

That all said, we are now entering uncharted territory. Our generation may be among the first in recent American history to have to face a future without the promise of Social Security in our senior years and, for that reason alone, the future is something we have to start planning for now. In the prime of your life, you may not be able to picture yourself being 62 years old, ready for retirement. But how much harder is it to picture yourself at 65, still having to work for a living?

You lay the foundation for your future early in life. Educate yourself about finances and be responsible for and realistic about your economic choices. Delaying instant gratification can lead to financial independence. Which one would you rather do: get a life or lease a lifestyle?

Learning the Basics

In a world where you can get married and divorced all in one weekend in Vegas (just ask Britney Spears!), it's hard to understand just how long "long-term" is. As a rule of thumb, long-term savings or investments are held for many years, without the intention of cashing them in or disposing of them in the near future. Picture a giant padlock on your favorite ATM.

One of the most basic savings techniques—and a good place to begin—is a common savings account, providing that you make regular, consistent deposits and limit your withdrawals. You may experience "shopping withdrawals," but you'll thank me later.

Once the deposit goes into your savings account, consider it off-limits to yourself. Put aside enough money from each paycheck to live on without depriving yourself entirely of everything you enjoy (we're talking monetary sense, not joining a monastery). Then stick to your budget and save up for more expensive potential purchases. This will give you a feeling of really having earned them and will also give you time to consider whether or not you really want them.

TIP! Using on-line banks like ING or Emigrant Direct often gives you substantially higher interest rates than most "brick and mortar" banks. Plus it takes a day or two to withdraw your money so you won't make as many impulsive purchases.

Spending all your money on CDs is a bad idea. Putting your money *into* CDs (Certificates of Deposit) is a good idea. It's the difference between listening to a rock star and *living like one.*

CDs are a special kind of savings account in which the initial money that you put in becomes inaccessible to you for a specified period of time. If you take it out before that, you pay a penalty. However, the interest paid on CDs is higher than that for a regular savings account, usually by three or four times. Put in whatever you can feasibly afford to ($2,000 is a good sum for starters) and forget about it until the time period is up (five years is a nice number that even the most commitment-phobic people can commit to without hyperventilating). When that amount of money becomes available again, it will have grown up right along with you.

The U.S. Securities and Exchange Commission website explains investing in CDs (and the compound interest you'd earn) like this: If a high school kid bought a piece of pizza for $2 every week, by the time she retired, she'd have spent $5,200 on pizza (and that's not including the cans of Coke). If she gave up that slice each week, besides being better for her skin, her parents could put that money into a long-term, high-yield CD instead (at 8% interest) and she'd have almost $65,000 waiting for her when she retires. That's the drastic difference between saving and spending.

Now, imagine if that same girl charged those slices of pizza and only paid the minimum balance each month. With the 20% interest rate on many credit cards, she'd be middle-aged before being able to pay it all off in full, plus it would wind up costing around $17,000—more than the down payment would be to buy her own pizzeria!

In addition to CDs, there are also a number of stocks known for their stability and slow, steady growth rates, as well as company-sponsored savings plans such as Individual Retirement Accounts (IRAs) and 401(k)s that are excellent long-term options. None of these are fancy solutions or require financial genius. They are simply ways to save for your future—and save yourself some serious problems. This is a really important topic, so rest assured that this isn't the last you're going to hear about ways to save! I'll go into it in more detail later on in the book. But no matter how "unsexy" talking about saving seems, know that your 30-year-old self will thank your 20-year-old self for having had the good sense not to have blown the entire bank account on useless stuff that only seemed important at the time. Now, if only the same thing could be said for having gotten that tattoo…

More to Life Than Money

You may have first seen me on *The Apprentice* but, of course, my story doesn't start there, just as it didn't end there. No journey to self-discovery ever begins so clearly, nor is it ever really complete.

In fact, my life has been more influenced by a book than by a TV show. As I was growing up, I had the good fortune to come across Herman Hesse's *Siddhartha* and found in its pages a story that reflected my own. Siddhartha is a young man who, stripped of worldly possessions, starts a journey to find himself and a higher meaning. He knows there are only two possible outcomes: either he'd find true bliss or he'd come back disillusioned with the world.

Along the way, he is tempted by possessions and lust—not to mention enormous wealth. Sound familiar? In the end, though, he is brought back to the river of his youth where he realizes that the true peace he had been seeking was actually within him all along.

All of my diverse experiences have led me to the same conclusion: The source of happiness is found within your own self. Everything else is just a search, even if it does take you to the most unimaginable places. Each distinct step of my life has imparted invaluable lessons to me that I adopted into my worldview and relied on to end up where I am today. I found bliss—but never lost sight of where I started.

Marketing and business are in my blood, so at a fairly young age I was able to determine what my passions and callings were. Yes, they made me wealthy—but, more importantly, they made me happy. To find your way in life, you must first find yourself. Whatever you decide are the main goals in your life, your career or your overall purpose, remember the words of Siddhartha: "The true profession of man is to find his way to himself." Everything else is just a job. It may satisfy your needs or wants, but it won't satisfy your soul.

As I grew up, my dreams of success, independence and financial freedom never changed, although my circumstances often did. The lesson? I knew myself best—my dedication, my capabilities, my desires—so I set my own goals and never wavered. I learned at an early age how easily everything could change. But that didn't change me. I counted on myself to make my dreams *my reality.*

I realize that in today's society, spending equals sexy. Think of the shoes, the clothes, the accessories you could charge! Retail has replaced relationships for personal satisfaction. With Calvin wrapped around you, Marc on your arm and Jimmy at your feet, who would want the spending to ever end?

Despite the glamorous TV shows and movies that look like ads with all their product placements or the exciting ads that look like movies with all their celebrity endorsers, keep in mind that that isn't how real life works. No matter what TV shows tell you, shoes aren't empowering. Setting a goal for yourself and working hard to reach it is.

Not Just A Lesson—A Lifestyle

Ironically, *saving* money is a lot like *losing* weight. Both take self-discipline to resist the temptation of immediate gratification, either in the form of food or stuff. Both budgets and diets only work if you stick to them for a long time, make a lifestyle change rather than a temporary concession, and don't cheat. (Hmm…come to think of it, this comparison could even be about making relationships work!) Anyway, setting out in the economic world is an uncertain and scary experience. It's like stepping on a scale: a lot of Americans aren't ready for what they have to face.

Step #1: Ask yourself what indulgences you can cut out of your life. Maybe it's as simple as not buying the tabloid magazine in the Target check-out aisle.

Instead of trying to create your identity by mirroring a celebrity, athlete or anyone else, concentrate on (and write down) ten things that define you. Who are you? What do you want from life? What do you love? What do you want to be? This shouldn't involve "stuff"—this is intangible identity. Things you want to own and belongings you have do not make you who you are. Don't let things become your identity because objects can be replicated and purchased by anyone. But YOU are unique!

CHAPTER TWO

RECOGNIZE POTENTIAL

Honey, We Shrunk the Class

Over the last few years, the American middle class has been shrinking. The comfortable lifestyle that so many workers aspire to is slipping through their fingers and being replaced by the widest gap between the rich and poor in modern history—with the majority getting caught on the wrong side of that line.

For the first time in America, young adults today are entering a society in which large numbers of

I CAN'T AFFORD TO ABSORB THE OVERHEAD
ANYMORE!

people are *exiting*—rather than entering—the middle class. In order to stay competitive in an increasingly globalized market, companies are cutting back salaries and eliminating benefits (only 60% offer health insurance), and the cost of living is far outpacing wage increases. Middle-class families' incomes have fallen in thirty-nine states and an estimated 14 million professionals will lose their job in the next few years as companies outsource an ever-increasing number of jobs overseas.

These are some alarming statistics. But unfortunately, that's the bleak business landscape that today's grads are entering. The old model of going to college, getting good grades, finding a stable job and eventually retiring on your pension just isn't the way it works anymore. This is why it's extremely important to start exploring new opportunities now.

Rethinking the Old Model

Students are graduating from college and, according to a study by the College Placement Council, the majority are finding entry-level work in fields that are not even related to their majors. All that school work for nothing! How many people do you know who have a four-year college degree and ended up with the exact kind of job they had before they graduated? On top of that, most of them start out with boatloads of student loans and credit card debt to pay off. Not a good start to that "promising future" most schools promise you.

I have a ton of friends who tried to tackle a four-year school tuition (often with their parents' help)

Taking Classes or Simply Taking Up Space?

"Students who cannot follow complex arguments accurately, yet are sitting in college classrooms, are not really learning. They are taking away a mishmash of half-understood information and outright misunderstandings that leave them under the illusion that they know something they do not."

— *Charles Murray, W.H. Brady scholar at the American Enterprise Institute*

and are still trying to climb their way out from under the crushing weight of student loans. They took whatever job was readily available just to get a weekly paycheck, no matter how unrelated it was to their educational major. Now they're stuck. And they're not alone.

However, there are also a lot of successful people who chose to abandon their fields of study when they realized that their real interests—and the chance at a real payoff—lay elsewhere. Can you imagine Federal Reserve chairman Alan Greenspan dealing with bands and rock instead of bonds and stock? His college major was music. Colin Powell graduated high school with a C average and decided to major in geology because "I got to study rocks!" He admitted that it was his real-world experience in the ROTC that first taught him the self-discipline he needed to succeed. And it's doubtful that instead of all those Barnes and Nobles bookstores he founded, Steve Riggio would have amassed the same fortune with his original major by opening a string of Anthropology 'R Us chain stores.

In the business world, the degree that matters most is your degree of commitment to what you are trying to achieve. After all, your degree doesn't say anything about you—but your know-how speaks volumes.

As this chart from *cnnmoney.com* shows, the commitment you put into education isn't necessarily

---

WORKING *REALLY* HARD FOR THE MONEY

Here are just a few careers where the time and money invested to qualify for a position can be disproportionately high to the pay.

	ANNUAL EARNINGS
Archaeologist	$38,620
Architect	$34,000 for first year intern; $68,900 for Senior architect
Chef	$9.86-$19.13 an hour
Clergy	$39,900
Assistant professor, liberal arts	$44,300
School psychologist	$51,170
University research scientist	
• Microbiologist	$39,100-$67,420*
• Medical	$35,520
• Social	$51,280

*Reflects the range of what the middle 50 percent of earners make. Otherwise, figures represent median earnings. Sources: Bureau of Labor Statistics (BLS), Salary.com, American Institute of Architects. BLS numbers reflect pay in 2002.

Cramming Our Colleges

"Properly understood, a four-year college education teaches advanced analytic skills and information at a level that exceeds the intellectual capacity of most people. If you want to do well in college and come away with a genuine, thorough education, you should have an IQ of 115 or higher. Put another way, it makes sense for only about 15% of the population, 25% if one stretches it, to get a college education. And yet more than 45% of recent high school graduates enroll in four-year colleges."

— *Charles Murray*

commensurate with what you'll earn afterwards. Plus the average student is going to graduate from four years of college $25,000 in the hole even with a couple of scholarships and a part-time job to partially pay off loans (*triple* that number for students who attend grad school). All that expense and hard work for a degree that gives you what? Teacher: $25,000 starting salary. Nurse: $35,000. Psychology major: a part-time job to earn enough money for grad school...or quit and analyze the customers as you bus their tables. None of these options come close to the $60K that many entrepreneurs and businesspeople *start off with*—even without a college degree!

A recent story in *Newsweek* entitled "The Lessons I Didn't Learn in College" was written by an academically successful grad who took a job as a cocktail waitress in a bowling alley in order to make ends meet. She admits that, despite her 3.9 GPA, she had trouble filling out a W-4 form because she had no idea about the fundamentals of personal finance. "My friends and I are graduates of Wesleyan, Barnard, Stanford and Yale," she writes, "…yet none of us knows what a Roth IRA is or can master a basic tax form." She guessed at the answers for her allowances and exemption claims and hoped for the best—a tactic that might work in school but could cost you plenty in the real world. Her conclusion was something I've been saying all along: There's a huge discrepancy between what students learn in school and what they need to know in the business world.

I'd like to illustrate that the stigma of "not going to school" is no longer a detriment in today's economic field. In fact, it sometimes shows good financial sense.

College Classes vs. Social Classes

"No data tells us what proportion of students really want four years of college-level courses, but it is safe to say that most are there to improve their chances of making a good living. What many really need is vocational training. But nobody will say so because 'vocational training' is considered 'second class.'"

— *Charles Murray*

My best friend, Beth, was the one to take me under her wing in high school when I first returned from Mexico. I hadn't been to an actual school in over seven years so I was a mess to say the least. Beth helped me out, even though she wasn't the greatest student in the world (she won't mind me saying that!). When we were in our senior year, we met with student counselors who spoke to each of us about our futures. I told mine I didn't want to go to college since there were other avenues I wanted to pursue with that time…and I think I nearly gave him a heart attack when I said that! Beth said she wasn't sure she wanted to try the college route either.

Beth and I both took a lot of heat from our other friends, who told us that we'd both become nobodies

Why Shakespeare 101 Won't Save Our Economy

"A large number of students on today's campuses are looking for something that the four-year college was not designed to provide. They want practical courses, but most of these specialties do not require four years of training, and the best way to teach those skills is not through an academic institution with the staff and infrastructure of a college, which is all so ridiculously inefficient."

— *Charles Murray*

A Small Degree of Difference

"Most college degrees are simply a screening device for employers: The college you got into says a little about your ability, and that you stuck with it for four years says something about your perseverance. But a bachelor's degree in many fields, such as business or economics, certifies nothing."

— *Charles Murray*

and live in poverty if we didn't follow the traditional route of higher education. That shook us up a little, so one night Beth came over and we figured it out for ourselves. We calculated the cost of tuition to go to college to become a teacher vs. not going to school and continuing work as a Montessori teacher at $13 an hour (which was what Beth was doing at the time). The difference was huge. Ten years down the line, if she stayed in that job with only incremental pay raises, she'd be better off than attending college, going into debt and making a measly $24,000 salary. School bus drivers are making more than teachers, with no student loans hanging over their heads! The point is that you really have to take a hard look at the numbers and not overestimate the value of a piece of paper you get from some school.

By the way, Beth is one of the best budgeters ever. She has more in her savings account than most

Fix the System

"The demand for college is market-driven, because a college degree does open access to certain jobs that are closed to people without one. The fault lies in the false premium that our culture has put on a college degree. The good news is market-driven systems eventually adapt to reality, and signs of change are already visible in career training institutes and two-year schools. They are more honest than four-year colleges about what their students want, and they provide courses that meet their needs more explicitly. The time frame of a two-year training course gives students a big advantage—two years is about right for learning many technical specialties, while four years is unnecessarily long...and exceptionally lucrative for the college!"

— *Charles Murray*

40-year-olds, doesn't have any debt and has gotten a great, highly respected job in a hospital after getting her license by attending a nine-month certification program. As for our friends, many of them have not yet found a "real job" after graduating college and they are still trying to pay off their loans by working as waiters/waitresses, bartenders or at retail stores.

According to a poll from *USA Today,* recent college grads fear getting deeper in debt (32.4%) and being unemployed (31.2%) more than they fear another terrorist attack (13.4%). And they have good reason to feel this threat from closer to home. If student loan rates keep rising at the current pace, they could end up paying 8.25% interest within a few years. That means, with the average student graduating anywhere from $10,000 to $20,000 in debt, it could take them at least another twenty-five years to pay off their loans—that is, if they're even lucky enough to find a job with a starting salary of $35K. Most college grads' work experience consists only of part-time service-industry jobs squeezed in between tightly packed

Using Your Head—and Your Hands

"The value of a college degree is being challenged since the spread of wealth at the top of American society has created an explosive demand for craftsmanship. Finding a good lawyer or physician is easy. Finding a good carpenter, painter, electrician or plumber is difficult, and it's a seller's market! Skilled craftspeople can routinely make six figures. They have work even in a soft economy. Their jobs cannot be outsourced to India. And their job provides rewards that come from mastering challenging skills that produce tangible results. How many white-collar, college-degree jobs can we say that about?"

— *Charles Murray*

class schedules. And with white-collar jobs being the new export earmarked for outsourcing overseas, careers in fields such as IT, manufacturing, computer sciences, engineering and financial services are decreasing, while chances of unemployment and underemployment are increasing along with the competition pool. It's no wonder that the *Today Show* recently reported that 60% of college grads are moving back home.

Compare the college student loan scenario with the alternative of attending a trade school

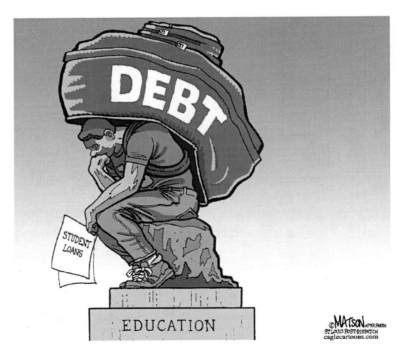

where the tuition is often one-third of a state university. Students can graduate with less debt and, after about two years of apprenticeship, are likely to get a job that doesn't pay as much as a white-collar career but at least ensures steady work providing an essential service. If everything works out well, student loans and any debts accrued during apprenticeship can be paid off in about ten years' time—that is, not including the mortgage!

Now compare both of these schooling options with going straight into the business world after high school. You'd have zero student loans and be making a sizable salary in the time it takes your peers to graduate—plus you'd have already gained enough experience to make youindispensable to your company or eminently hireable to another one, putting you

Education Without the Expense

"Even though foregoing college makes a lot of economic sense, the social stigma remains. That will erode only when large numbers of high-status, high-income people do not have a college degree—and don't care! The information-technology industry sets some good examples with Bill Gates and Steve Jobs."

— *Charles Murray*

School's Out!

"In business and technology, the importance to present an employer with evidence that you are good at something, even without a college degree, will continue to increase. Every time that happens, the false premium our society attaches to four-year colleges will diminish."

— *Charles Murray*

ahead of the competition. On top of that, with no student debts to pay off, you'd have the possibility to add to your earned income with investments in real estate, stocks and bonds (a lot more on that in the next chapters). In the time it takes college grads just to repay loans and break even, you could amass a huge amount of savings. Profits from property investments? $250,000. Stocks? $100,000 and counting. Never having to worry about moving back in with your parents? Priceless.

Now, I'm not trying to paint a picture that continuing education is bad, because it's not. Young adults just really need to evaluate why they are going to school, what they are going for, and how they can make the most of it.

Forbes figured out that the cost of a top-quality education is $144,000 for four years. If that

money was instead invested into an average municipal bond at just 5%, you would have a nice nest egg by your mid-30s and, by retirement, it would mature into $500,000—far more than the average college grad would be able to save by working all that time.

A $40K Kegger

So why will many campuses remain overstocked for such a long time to come? The answer is simple: "Most students find college life to be lots of fun— apart from that boring classroom stuff."

— *Charles Murray*

Motivated thinkers can teach themselves almost anything through apprenticeships, internships or the Internet. The old "get a formal education then slowly work your way up the corporate ladder" formula is on the way out. Things move more quickly in this day and age. Innovation and ingenuity are more valuable commodities in the business world than the ability to write research papers or memorize information by rote.

The number of young people who get out of college, send out some résumés, and go to work in retail or at a restaurant to pay off their debt is

Hi-Tech Teachers

"Advances in technology are making brick-and-mortar college facilities increasingly irrelevant. Research resources on the Internet will soon make university libraries unnecessary; lecture courses taught by first-rate professors are already available on CDs and DVDs; and advances in computer simulation are expanding the skills that can be taught without having to gather students together in a laboratory or classroom. In short, the cost of complete, effective training can fall for anyone who is willing to give up the trappings of a campus."

— Charles Murray

appalling. They have been systematically pro-grammed to sell themselves short. The funny thing is, when I talk to friends about all the opportunities that exist to start their own business, create some-thing new or invest, they stare at me cluelessly, scared out of their minds to take a chance on doing something different that their teachers didn't tell them about. It's like they'd rather be poor because it seems easier to do what's expected, swipe their credit cards and slowly pay them off in installments. But life is not on an installment plan!

But is it really worth paying over $40,000 for a four-year party?!

Creating New Opportunities

I have nothing against higher education, but I think I really need to hit my readers hard with, well, reality! This generation is seriously living in la-la land if we don't realize that we have to break the daze with some new modes of thinking that reflect the fast-paced, modern society we live in. Degrees don't guarantee success.

Don't believe me? Ask Bill Gates, Larry Ellison (the cofounder of database giant Oracle), Alan Gerry (who started the first cable TV network and sold it to Time Warner for $2.8 billion) or John Simplot (the inventor of frozen french fries)—all of whom created successful opportunities for themselves without a college degree. Add me to that list, too. If you frame it, a degree may fill an empty space on your wall...but it doesn't necessarily fill a business with the best-qualified people!

The surest way to financial success is not to just think outside the box, but to destroy the box altogether. There should be no limits on new ways of thinking.

Think outside the cage...and business will soar!

Bucking Tradition

Let's look at one example of out-of-the-box thinking that was right there in front of us all along—in our car cupholders and on our kitchen counters. Yet it took one person's different way of seeing that morning cup of coffee, which has since become almost synonymous with the name Starbucks, to turn a low-priced item into an incredibly lucrative industry.

Starbucks started as a local storefront shop in Seattle, where it quickly gained a reputation as

serving some of the best coffee in the area. But beyond opening a few small branches nearby, their potential for growth seemed limited in a market already dominated by some nationally recognized names that could serve coffee (as well as other food items) faster and cheaper—the two basic requirements of caffeine-addicted consumers.

The problem the company faced was that their product was nothing new. The solution, then, was to change the way coffee was being seen by—and sold to—customers.

Howard Schulz, Starbucks' marketing executive, was on vacation in Italy, where he was inspired by the Italian espresso bar and how both coffee in itself and the concept of coffee breaks were ingrained in the culture as a part of everyday life—and an escape from it. While Americans were traditionally used to thinking about coffee as something you get on the go to keep you going, there was an entirely different way of looking at it, like the English institution of afternoon tea.

Schulz convinced the founders of Starbucks to open a coffee bar where the relaxed ambience and café-inspired décor were actually parts of the product being sold. No American in their right mind would pay $4 for a cup of coffee, but they would pay $4 for a comfortable place to sit, talk and take a break from their hectic days. For that total experience, $4 felt like a bargain.

Once that first prototype proved successful, the founders got local investors to believe in their innovative vision and fund the company's expansion—which is in evidence on street corners in almost every city in America and over thirty countries worldwide. Starbucks' success is based on a lot more than lattes—it is the result of reconceptualizing an already popular and proven product and recognizing its potential for growth. Who knew a cuppa joe could be worth a cuppla million?

Putting Technology to Work

Another way to create opportunities is by developing a product or service to meet your own needs and fill a hole in the market. Everybody has had the thought, "I wish there were a product out there that could..." but only true entrepreneurs act on it.

The idea that one product, which hasn't yet been introduced into mass consciousness, would make everyone's life a little easier has served as a business inspiration time and again. The trick is to take this idea out of your own mind-set and put it into the hands of consumers. And the tool is often technology.

In 1995, computer programmer Pierre Omidyar was doing what practically every other person in his profession was preoccupied with: obsessing over the Internet and what some of its practical and personal applications could be. With a few established companies already seeing huge success with on-line shopping, Omidyar had some notion that technology and consumerism went hand-in-hand but it was over dinner with his fiancé that this idea really "clicked."

Of all things, she was an avid collector of PEZ dispensers, the little bobble-headed toys that clicked out candy. The couple had just moved and she was having trouble finding collectibles traders near their new neighborhood. Omidyar realized the solution to what they had both been looking for.

He went home and wrote the computer code for what would later become *eBay*, the innovative Internet service that connects consumers with sellers all over the world. It's now a household name—fusing the latest technology with the time-honored tradition of garage sales.

eBay's multimillion dollar profits (that's a lot of PEZ dispensers!) came from Omidyar's ability to recognize a need, provide a service and use existing technology in the sale of products that other people already owned. What's being sold is beside the point; the innovation is in how it's being sold. The Internet has opened up a whole new world of opportunities for service-based businesses and intrepid entrepreneurs.

Lessons Learned

What these two examples show is that you don't have to reinvent the wheel in order to have a viable product or service. What you do need is the ability to recognize potential and make it a reality. We live in a consumer-driven society, so people are always willing to spend some money on quality items that are uniquely marketed or useful services that are easily accessible. Whether success comes from changing the way consumers see a certain product or

A Piece of Paper Doesn't Prove Anything

"A college degree itself does not actually qualify the graduate for anything."

Charles Murray

utilizing your experience and expertise to provide an innovative, user-friendly service, it all starts with identifying a single goal.

At a rather young age, I set my mind toward economic independence. I learned early on that having a specific goal was the first step in reaching financial fulfillment and self-reliance. Every action I took was a means toward that end—even selling porcupine quills, as odd as that may seem…but then again, think of the pet rock!

Ideally, your work should incorporate your passions—and your passions should encompass your

"Looks like a white flag."

whole heart. But I knew even back then, as most people know, that a little more money would have made things a whole lot easier.

Financial stress was the reason my family lost everything we had in the first place. In fact, 75% of Americans identify money as the chief source of stress in their lives. But it doesn't have to be that way—money is actually supposed to help relieve some stress in your life by making things a bit easier!

There are ways to make money work for you by investing in your own future, keeping your mind open to opportunities and looking for the potential in unexpected places.

Inner Resources and Running Water

I learned all about hidden human potential in— of all places—a humble water pump!

When my family first pulled up to our mobile home property in the middle of the Wisconsin woods, it was the first day of January—a new beginning. It was also 40 degrees below zero and we didn't have any electricity or gas lines. There was no running water and no working restroom.

It was about as bare-boned as anyone could imagine in this day and age. I felt like I was actually living in one of the history lessons that I learned back in school.

Just getting to the house meant a two-and-a-half-hour drive from St. Paul, Minnesota along dirt roads, some of which were plowed, if we were lucky. As our car wound through the thick trees, I remember looking up at the sky and watching the telephone lines and electricity wires disappear. It seemed, with each mile, that we were getting further away from civilization. As we drove, I didn't see any other houses near-by, only an occasional hunting shack. Let's just say we were reaching a new level of isolation.

The mobile home that my parents purchased was what is known in the real estate business as a real "fixer upper." In everyday English, that trans-lates to something like a "trash heap." At that time, my mother was pregnant with my fourth sibling, so she couldn't do any physical labor on our land. I was the oldest of the children and, as such, was given the most responsibility. So when my mom and brothers and sisters went to stay with my aunt, I stayed at the mobile home with my father, making our new house, if not hos-pitable, at least inhabitable.

First things first, we had to have water. To do that, we drilled at least 10 holes for water into the frozen ground but came up empty each time. Just to have bath water, we'd have to break a hole in the ice that covered the river every morning then carry the heavy buckets filled with water up to the house to heat on the wood stove. Yes, those things really still exist in the age of the microwave.

My dad drilled all day long for weeks in order to find a source of water that we could use to make a well. And I'm not talking about a gas or electric drill...I mean hand drilling. Picture an old-fashioned corkscrew opener—but much, much larger and heavier—twisting into fifty feet of solid earth instead of a wine bottle. I'd help my father maneuver this unwieldy device and start a large fire over each drilling spot to soften the soil. When we finally reached an underground spring, it meant that we'd have running water. It also ended up tasting terrific! Performing those tasks is when I truly learned the value of H2O, human sweat and discovering what was hidden to others. It wasn't a very easy existence for a young girl. But looking back, I realize it had its advantages. When my whole family finally moved into the home that we refurbished with our own unrelenting labor, I felt the sense of pride and accomplishment that only comes from a job well done.

Relying only on ourselves, we were able to build something where, before, there had only been unyielding, empty ground—and unseen potential. We tapped into hidden resources both literally, in the underground well, and personally, into our inner strength.

That kind of difficult work afforded me the opportunity to picture what I could achieve and to bring it to completion. It's something I never lost sight of in the world of business: Have a vision and see the potential where no one else does. Then use your own two hands to make it come to life.

Goal Tending

Setting goals for yourself programs your mind to actively move toward achievement. By knowing exactly what it is that you want to happen, your thoughts will automatically focus in that direction and your efforts will be aimed toward the desired outcome.

True success can only be achieved if you set goals that reflect your own values and wants. Basing your goals on a desire to please others—your parents, friends, significant other or even social expectations at large—will never leave you satisfied, even if you obtain them. So it's not just about picking the "right" goals, but knowing which ones are right for you.

But it's also not enough to have vague goals like "I want to be happy" or "I want to be rich." First of all, who doesn't? And secondly, those words have different meanings to different people. What is your definition of happiness and how financially successful would you have to be in order to have a feeling of security and satisfaction?

In order to be meaningful for you, goals should be specific. Really think in detail about what it is you'd like to accomplish. The more details you provide, the easier it will be to visualize success—to actually see yourself in the place or circumstances that you want to create.

Goals should be measurable, meaning that you can identify each step that you will need to take in order to attain them. That also means that they should be realistic and actually achievable, otherwise you're doomed from the start. Now, I'm not saying that success can't happen beyond your wildest dreams...it did for me. I'm just saying that you shouldn't set yourself up for failure, which can be internalized and block your way toward achieving goals that are within your grasp. Want to be financially independent? That's very possible. Want it to happen overnight in one lump sum? Then there better be a lottery machine close-by.

On the other hand, goals should be challenging enough that, if you really want to achieve them, you'll have to push yourself, be prepared to make some sacrifices along the way—and know that it'll all be worth it in the end.

CNNMoney.com did an article on "What It Takes to Be Great." It said that according to scientists, it's not so much that certain people are born with innate abilities or talents as it is a matter of practicing to attain skill sets and realize goals. They call this "deliberate practice" and it's what separates the best in any field from the rest of the competition. Deliberate practice is any activity that's specifically designed to improve performance and help you reach for objectives that are just beyond your level. The example they give is this: Most golfers don't get any better by just hitting balls by the bucket because that's not a deliberate exercise. However, "hitting an eight-iron three hundred times with a goal of leaving the ball within twenty feet of the pin 80% of the time, continually observing results and making appropriate adjustments, and doing that for hours every day—

that's deliberate practice." It's the same for business as it is in sports. The more specific you are in your goals, the better able you are to concretely ascertain what it takes to achieve them. Then, of course, it's just a matter of perfecting your swing.

You'll also need to focus on the obstacles that stand between you and each one of your goals. This is a strategy-building technique. If you are able to identify the things that are likely to get in your way, you'll be more likely to find ways around them. Recognizing a potential obstacle before you encounter it is the surest way to overcome it. You should also set projected target dates for the completion of each goal, keeping in mind that some achievements take longer than others. Checkpoints will help to keep you on the right track and cut down on frustration or the temporary temptation to give up.

With the obstacles identified and a timetable in place for each goal, it's time to begin the real work. On a piece of paper, you should write down each goal you have set for yourself. Create a chart that shows where you are now, where you plan to be within a given time frame, what obstacles are likely to get in your way and how you will get around them. Every journey needs a road map and these charts will be your guide to get you closer to successfully achieving your goals.

Every day, ask yourself what actions you can take that will move you one step closer toward completing your goal. Then break those actions down into specifics—and do them. Is there someone who would be beneficial to talk to, to get information from or assist you on your way? Did you make an appointment to talk to that person? If not, pick up the phone. Is there a book you could be reading that would help you understand the process better? If so, have you gotten that book? Yes? Well, have you gotten through the first chapter? Is there a class you could take, a seminar you could attend, a web site you can visit? How many of those things did you do today? How many will you do tomorrow?

My Immediate Goals:
Where I Am Now:
Where I Want To Be in Six Months:
How to Get There:
Obstacles I Must Overcome:
Where I Want To Be in One Year:

If you're serious about success, these are the steps you need to take to make it tangible. No one said being successful would be easy or quick—and if *anyone* did, well, they lied. It requires hard work every day. I believe that too many Americans feel that they are entitled to wealth because they live in a rich country, but they have no desire to work for it. We must reprogram ourselves to not only be willing to work, but to seek out ways to better ourselves even if it's difficult. You may not be the most talented or educated, but you can *always* be the hardest worker—and the hardest worker *always* succeeds. I'm an example of that.

As silly as it may sound, I used to write down my goals and life plan daily—on any surface available. I'd write them on my mirror, then in my shower, then in crayon on my walls. They were constant reminders and encouragement to myself that no matter how hard I was struggling to achieve them at that time or how many people didn't believe in me, my goals were always within reach.

I knew I could make my dreams a reality if I kept pushing myself toward my vision of success. And that vision was everywhere I could see it…whether I was brushing my teeth at night or making breakfast in the morning.

That first house became a testament in itself to achieving my goals when I bought it at 19 years old. There is so much emotion packed into its walls that it's hard for me to articulate it. It's so overwhelming to me that just writing this now is making me tear up, thinking about the many nights I stayed awake inside it, deciding exactly what I wanted out of life and how I would make it all happen. That house was the first real thing I owned in this world—a symbol that my hard work was paying off and that I was becoming who I wanted to be.

I still own the house, with the crayoned goals and dreams written on its walls, and I keep it as a personal remembrance—whenever I walk through it, reading the rainbow of writing—that anything is possible if you continually strive toward your goals, despite any obstacles that may seem to be in your way. I found out that you can be who you want to be—just don't give up and become what everyone else is expecting.

Step #2: Analyze your opportunities. What are your talents? What could you do with them? What would satisfy your soul? Write down your goals— and don't ever sell yourself short. Once you set your goal and construct a plan to achieve it, roll up your sleeves and get working on it. There is nothing more satisfying than setting a goal, working hard and finally achieving it.

CHAPTER THREE

FOCUS ON— AND FINANCE— YOUR GOALS

Fine Tuning

So, did you figure it out yet? What do you want from your life? Two hundred thousand dollars in your savings account by next year? Your own pet store? Want to retire in three years? A fifty-unit apartment building that makes you $20,000 a month? Want to be out of debt by the end of the year? Send your kids to college so they don't have to worry about loans? Buy your dream house in Maui? Travel the world for a year? Do you want to be on the cover of *Forbes* with your own invention? You can.

But once you've figured out what your goals are in business and in life, it isn't always easy to stay focused or find the financing to stand on your own two feet. In order to go after your goals fully and dedicate yourself to your own vision of yourself, you must first overcome the limitations placed on all of us by prepackaged ways of thinking and the internal and external expectations that can, if you allow them, become the roadblocks to your success.

Self-Interest and Financial Interest

I know it's easy to say, "Go out and achieve your goals" but, if you were like me when I first started writing down goals, mine felt like they were simply pipe dreams with no possibility of me attaining them. I'd write down "Become a millionaire by the time I'm 30," but I had no idea what that actually entailed, let alone how the heck I was going to get there.

That's why, in the next three chapters, I'm going to break down what was really the structure of all of my dreams, which took me a while to discover. I've read a lot of books, listened to motivational tapes, but I never felt like there was a "how to" guide for accomplishing my goals. Everyone has an opinion or a hypothesis, like "One Minute Millionaire" or "Keys to Your Financial Freedom." But did anyone ever become a millionaire in a minute or have someone else hand them the keys? To be honest, after all that, I'd become even more confused and nowhere closer to my goal. So I'm not saying that what you'll read in the next few chapters will reveal all these secrets because there aren't any secrets! To sum it up, it's about working your butt off and understanding the streams of income.

We are going to go over earned income, passive income and portfolio income, and you will find that one or another will help you reach your goal. Whether you want to travel all the time or you want to retire when you're young, it's your understanding of these origins of income and how to achieve them that will take you to the next level financially. You take care of the "working your butt off" part, and I'll share with you a way to direct your focus so that you will be able to accomplish your goals and dreams. Sound fair? Good. Because becoming a millionaire, retiring young and owning a yacht are all in your future. You just need to want your goals bad enough and, most importantly, know the dynamics of how to get there.

Earned Income

Now let's start off with something you are probably all too familiar with: your J.O.B. Sadly, for many Americans, that translates into "Just Over Broke."

You work, you get paid; you work, you get paid; you stop working? Yep, you guessed it—you stop getting paid. Bummer.

Stop and think for a minute what would happen if you lost your job today. What do you have in savings? Is it enough to live on for a while and pay the bills? Do you have a second income? Hmm... I'm guessing no. So do you think you might need to have another source of income?

You better believe it because over the last year, the job market has slowed, keeping pace with the slumping economy. According to the Economic Policy Institute, during a six-month period in 2006, the monthly job growth fell to half of what it had been six months prior. With this kind of instability, the average JOE can no longer rely on his JOB.

The Economic Policy Institute reported that American jobs producing software recently fell by 128,000, while over 100,000 new jobs in that industry were created in India. Analysts also predict that 10% of U.S. legal work and 12% of accounting jobs will be outsourced, showing that many fields—from factory work to white-collar careers—will be affected. While these jobs will be lost to local employees, statistics show that most of them don't have significant savings to hold them over while they search for their next position in an ever-diminishing job market.

Wage growth has slowed sharply in order to keep up with overseas competitors and though employees can compensate by working longer hours, those hours simply aren't available anymore due to decreasing demand. So many businesses are in financial trouble that there's an up-to-the-minute on-line service that keeps track of companies on the brink of, or already in, bankruptcy. Among the hundreds of current listings are such major corporations and job suppliers as Calpine, Winn-Dixie, Parmalat, Delphi, Allied Holdings, and about half a dozen airlines—even two or three Trump buildings and casinos have filed Chapter 11. Even successful companies like Wal-Mart are implementing wage caps, cutting hours and using more part-time staff to keep prices competitive.

To this bleak economic climate, we can add the chilling loss of worker compensation. Like the disappearing Social Security program, employee benefits are on the endangered list. In many states, the maximum worker compensation rate is not enough to cover rent, let alone food, clothes and health care costs. The recent $9 million national reduction of employee benefits is the equivalent of 300 Americans losing $30,000 jobs.

In short, we are watching our jobs being outsourced! So, I'm going to ask you again: Do you think you need to create another source of earned income in your life?

Okay, before you answer that, let me ask you a few more questions:

Would you like to be your own boss?

Would you like to not have to rely solely on your paycheck from your job?

Would you like to get out of debt? Buy a new car? Go on vacation?

Would you like to not have to worry about losing your job to cheap overseas labor?

If you answered YES to any of the above, then let's start going over other sources of earned income.

The Entrepreneur

One common misconception many people have about entrepreneurship is that they think they have to quit their job cold turkey, armed with a bunch of capital and an elaborate business plan. The thing is that few businesses ever start off that way.

More often, they start out in someone's basement with some strong coffee and, perhaps most importantly, with a strong passion. The founders of Yahoo! started their enterprise between classes in a campus trailer, as a way to keep track of their personal interests on the Internet. At first, it was just something to distract them from their studies—until they realized the profit that could be made from their pet project.

There are countless stories of how a variety of multibillion-dollar businesses were born from humble beginnings—from search engines to skyscrapers—but they all have something in common: an entrepreneur who made it happen. You don't have to give up everything else in your life and hock everything you own in order to start a business and earn some extra income. After all, that's what most people go into business in order to avoid! The truth is that energy and creativity are the most important assets of any company. How much of those qualities you put into your business matters more than the capital you put in.

Want to earn good income in a bad job market? Becoming an entrepreneur allows you the opportunity to earn an income commensurate with your ambition without having to worry about job security. If you have the drive to sell your products or services, the opportunities you create for yourself can be unlimited!

Sure, it's natural to have reservations at first about making such a bold move as starting your own business. But what exactly are you afraid of losing? A job that may be outsourced at any moment? Dreams of a retirement that may never come? A stock option that might as well be paid out in monopoly money if your company is one of the many that file for bankruptcy? Starting your own business gives you something traditional jobs don't—control over your finances and your future.

If your goal, like mine, is financial freedom, nothing gives you more independence than generating income on your own.

Dream Small

I know, I know...Trump always says, "Dream big." And I definitely agree with Mr. Trump in most cases. But when you are thinking about starting your business, the biggest piece of advice I could give you is to stop dreaming for a second about the 25 manufacturing plants you'll have around the world, the 30,000 employees and your face on the front of *Forbes*. You *will* get there, but first you have to think in terms of baby steps:

First step: What kind of business do you want?
Second: Will you provide a product or a service?
Third: Who are your competitors?

Fourth: How will your product or service be different from your competitors'?

Fifth, and most importantly: Are you willing to work harder than anyone else to make this happen?

Starting Out Small

If you are starting out small, as most businesses do, it may be a good idea to know what the term "small business" actually means. A small business is an enterprise usually begun without the benefit of reserve finances and nurtured by an individual (or a handful of individuals) who are willing to work long hours and reinvest initial income to keep the business growing. It is critical at the beginning, when these two or three people find themselves doing the work of fifty, to already have established objectives in terms of marketing, delivery and financial success.

To be sure you're on solid financial ground before making the leap to open a small business, you need to think long-term. That requires cost analysis of how much you'll need to invest in your operation—not just to get it off the ground initially, but to keep it going for five to seven years. This is crucial, since, of the small businesses that do not succeed, 85% of them fail in the first five years. Don't lose hope—but do have a plan!

After a few unsuccessful attempts at starting his chocolate business, Milton Hershey was almost bankrupt by the time he was 30. He knew he had a great product but buyers weren't interested in a small-time operation that wouldn't be able to meet demand. In order to increase production but stay true to his original recipe, Hershey started staying up nights to make chocolate so he could focus exclusively on sales during the day. The result? Sweet success!

Sam Walton's first store in Newport, Arkansas, failed to make money for him long before Wal-Mart became a national institution and household name. With his next attempt, he kept doors open long after competitors went home for the night and stayed there personally greeting each customer like a guest.

In both of these instances, accomplishment came through small shifts in the equation (changes in marketing and selling styles) and an infinite willingness to work for what you believe in. Sometimes it's that simple. The difference between success and failure comes down to working your butt off, putting your mind to it and pouring your whole heart into it—that's the "Anatomy of Economics."

The Will to Make It Work

Have you ever noticed how a lot of people you know come up with some really good ideas for products or services that they just never put into motion? We all have it in us. In fact, you can witness this phenomenon almost any time you watch late-night TV with friends. A commercial will come on for some product that seems both ingenious and obvious at the same time and someone will shout out, "They stole my idea!" I call this the "Swiffer Effect."

A lot of people have come up with pretty remarkable and commercially viable ideas and products that they simply don't know what to do with next. Chances are, they lost focus and the idea died a few short seconds after its brilliant beginnings. But if you're serious about succeeding in business, it's time to stop being like most people. Recognize and capitalize on remarkable ideas—otherwise someone else will.

In order to sell a product or service, you have to think seriously about the audience to which you want to market it. How will your idea appeal to them? Or rather than changing the nature of a service or coming up with a new product, you could also concentrate on ways in which the behavior of your target audience can be modified to fit your item.

Dating services are a good example of this. Certainly the patent to matchmaking doesn't actually belong to anyone...unless it's shared by meddling moms everywhere. But it's a product with built-in potential since the supply of singles is already abundant and the demand for dating is a constant. Yet the innovative idea of making on-line matches appealing and socially acceptable to technology-savvy professional singles who are hard-pressed for time (rather than hard-pressed to find dates) is what really sells those services. In order to get ideas like these off the ground, you have to know how to make them attractive, kind of like a personal profile.

No matter what product or service you focus on providing, it's impossible to convince consumers to pay for it until you're completely sure of how it can be used to make people's lives easier, better or more productive. You have to really think through all the specifics...more than that, write it all down in detail. Niche products and services often survive even the worst economic slumps.

It's equally important to thoroughly know your product and fully understand your consumer in order to reach the buying public. And in this way, marketing is everything.

Starting from Scratch

When I was about 16 years old, my family and I moved back to Minnesota (after a year and a half of missionary work in Monterrey, Mexico) to give life in the United States another try. It was like we were starting all over again; we had next to nothing, except the experiences earned with our own two hands in the woods of Wisconsin.

Because of the years spent on the farm and in Mexican orphanages with no recent proof of employment and no savings, my parents' struggle to secure a mortgage was intense. My grandparents still lived in Stillwater, Minnesota, so for the time being we stayed with them, living out of our suitcases for about four months while my father tried to restart his chiropractic business. Life was still far from settled.

With special permission from administrators at my new high school, I was able to get out of classes before noon each day to help my father with the construction of his clinic. I still had the expertise from my days as an "outhouse engineer," so building the front office desk, organizing treatment rooms and painting the walls seemed like child's play to me. We had the place looking like an office in no time and, in that short period, I had an epiphany. It occurred to me that each can of paint, every pencil, had a price tag and represented an investment in the business. My parents had been sure to make the relationship between expenses and profits abundantly clear: Everything we put into the clinic had to ensure that we'd make more out of it.

While that concept could seem almost overwhelming (getting pencils and paints was easy, but where do you get customers and how do you bring in revenue?), it actually seemed simple to me: I'd do whatever job had to be done, even the ones no one else wanted to do, and in that way build the business from the ground up.

My Dad taught me, through actions more than words, that there was no secret formula to making a business successful. It simply took hard work, discipline and a clear picture of the end results—a lesson I keep in mind even today.

My father decided to make me Office Manager and head of the Marketing Department (the "Marketing Department," by the way, was made up exclusively of me!). He also explained the basic chiropractic philosophy to me: how each part of the body functioned together holistically for greater well-being. I thought that lesson was a pretty good model for the principles of business.

Just like in the body, where the brain communicates down the spinal cord, through the vertebrae, out the nerves to every cell, tissue, muscle and organ, I made it my mission to spread the news of our business to everyone in the community.

In a relatively short time, I helped my father build the client base up to 700 patient visits per week. How? By basically working my butt off! We went door to door; I introduced myself to all the businesses in the area, handed out flyers at grocery stores, performed free spinal screenings, demonstrated massage techniques at malls. I did anything and everything I could think of to get our name out there and advertise our services, which was made much easier by the fact that I believed strongly in what I was doing. If you have a good product, I figure you owe it to the public to let them hear about it.

Persistence paid off. Though it's hard to believe, that's how I started out in my marketing career. I discovered my love of marketing and, in the process, spread the chiropractic philosophy throughout the community with so much success that within six months, my father opened a second clinic. He put me in charge of the front office operations—all this while I was a junior in high school.

By the end of junior year, while I was running my father's clinic, a lot of other doctors heard about our success and starting calling me for marketing advice. I couldn't believe it! My reputation for hard work and getting the job done spread by word of mouth and before long I was marketing for chiropractic clinics around the city. I suddenly felt like I was doing exactly what I was supposed to with my life and, better yet, I was becoming successful doing it.

My Motto: Don't Be Afraid to Look Ridiculous

You might feel silly passing out flyers to your friends, relatives and everyone you come in contact with advertising the bait-and-tackle shop that's set up in your garage, but that's okay because sooner than later, if you work hard, you'll have your own freestanding fishing and sporting shop that you've always dreamed of.

Start with what you have. If you want to introduce the next on-line networking portal, start building the web page and optimizing the site. If you want to someday compete with PETCO, start a specialty pet boutique in your basement and go door to door handing out doggy treats to let everyone know you mean business. There are tons of ways to get the word out about your product and create a buzz without blowing your entire savings account.

Years ago, inexpensive advertising consisted of sandwich boards or getting a guy inside a hot dog costume. Come to think of it, I still see both of these examples every time I visit Manhattan! New York notwithstanding, the term "guerilla marketing" is used to describe innovative and unique ways to bring your product directly to the public. Consider these examples:

Ben and Jerry's first opened in a renovated gas station in Vermont. To attract customers, they held free movie nights in the summer, projecting films directly onto their outside walls. And what goes better with a free film on a hot night than some cold ice cream in never-before-tasted flavors?

The two cofounders of Nantucket Nectars started out selling their product to a pretty captive audience. They'd fill up a boat with bottles of their fruit juices and row them out to thirsty sailors, soon becoming the 7-11 of the Seven Seas.

From passing out frisbees in a park (that you bought in bulk) with your company's website written on them, to getting a bunch of your friends to wear matching customized tees (with a clever saying and your website spelled out in iron-on letters) the next time you attend a sporting event, remember that marketing comes in many forms, from the ridiculous to the sublime. The point is not to simply introduce consumers to your product but to pique their interest and get them talking about it. And that's the kind of marketing that money can't buy.

Most Likely to Succeed

By the time graduation came around, I had already constructed a successful business from scratch—and it was showing no signs of stopping. So I couldn't imagine shutting it down to go to college when I was already getting the best business education I possibly could in the real world of competitive marketing.

I had not only learned the financial and organizational aspects of marketing inside and out (which I considered my major), I also had a good understanding of the fundamentals of chiropractic (my minor). Knowing your product is essential to selling it and, better yet, believing in it makes others believe as well. So one day a chiropractic student approached me with a business proposition combining the two: He wanted us to start a marketing company exclusively for chiropractic offices. It's what I knew best so I decided to give it a shot.

After high school ended, I put all of my efforts into this venture business and we started marketing for doctors all across the Twin Cities. As our success grew, my goal of financial independence became clearer and closer. At 19, my earned income was astronomically higher than that of other people my age. In fact, I was outearning the majority of chiropractors I worked with. But with business overhead, car costs and renting an apartment, I wouldn't meet my financial goals just by putting aside a percentage of my salary each week. Day-to-day spending was seriously cutting into my savings, so I knew I needed a new plan.

What I really wanted was economic independence doing something I truly loved. So when my partnership in chiropractic marketing began to sour, I left immediately rather than compromise what I knew to be right for me and started my own business, Exposure Marketing.

Then at 19 years old, I discovered my "blueprint plan," another important source of income: real estate.

Own a Piece of the American Dream

Owning and running my own little business was fantastic; the only problem was...I worked a ton. I loved what I did so it wasn't a problem, but at

19 years old I decided I wanted to start working smarter and creating another source of earned income in my life. I researched many avenues and the most appealing and lucrative one was real estate.

Real estate is a vast source of earned income since, unlike a lot of careers, American homes aren't being shipped overseas. For the individual, home ownership is an important source for building wealth and a vital piece in achieving the American Dream. In fact, the primary investment of most Americans is the ownership of a single family residence. The Federal Reserve reported the net worth of homeowners as $171,700 and for renters, only $4,800. Consumer spending affects the economy according to the rise and fall of equity, derived mainly from home ownership and the stock market. Yet, beyond economic measure, owning a home provides many intangible benefits for the individual and society: stability, security, shelter.

Although successful real estate investing isn't hard, it does require knowledge and training. I'm providing basic information to help you get started, but I strongly suggest that you obtain some professional training (as I did) before proceeding in depth. Many of my first mistakes could have been avoided with additional knowledge...and that doesn't include 20/20 hindsight. There are a lot of real opportunities to make serious money in real estate. There are also some real risks. They don't call it "real" estate for nothing!

Wholesale Housing

Certain types of real estate investments, such as wholesale housing, can produce significant earned income because they involve buying and selling existing properties to create an almost immediate cash flow. Although there are big financial benefits to wholesale housing, which used to be known by the less flattering description "prefab housing," there are also drawbacks in that finding available properties and qualified buyers takes a great deal of time and effort. Believe me, you will have definitely earned this earned income!

To begin with, you'll have to find the best sources for locating wholesale deals and that means looking beyond the usual multiple listing services since the majority of wholesale housing opportunities are available only through independent sellers. The advantage of this kind of real estate investment, however, is that your hard work will pay off handsomely. You can bring in more money on one wholesale housing deal than you may make in a month on rental properties or other types of real estate investments that take quite some time to show a profit.

Another advantage to this type of investment is that, according to a recent issue of *Money* magazine, despite the perceived cooling in the housing market, wholesale is the way to go. Some regions are still experiencing a double-digit growth in this real estate sector and *Money* maintains that they don't predict "a wholesale housing collapse" anytime in the near future. So wholesale makes a whole lotta sense!

Wholesale deals are a wonderful launching pad to get you started in investing because you can do them with very little money and you don't need to use your credit. The very basics are as follows:

Find the house—As mentioned earlier, you are not going to find profitable wholesale homes on the multiple listing service, so I recommend simply driving around local neighborhoods. Look for "For Sale by Owner" homes or properties that look less expensive than the other average homes in the neighborhood (that's the "rehab look"). After you spot one, write down the address.

Find the owner—There are a few different ways to do this:

A.) Talk to the neighbors. Most of the time, the homeowner does not live on the property, and more often than not it is vacant. So, trust me...the neighbors will give you the info on the homeowner if they have it.

B.) Check public records. Go to the county courthouse, or most states have this info available on-line. Get the property owner's name then look them up in the phone book.

C.) Use Skip Tracer. Google "Skip Tracer Report"—many will come up and I've found that you don't have to pay more than $10 to get the info you need.

Call and negotiate with the owner—You will find that most buyers are happy to speak with you. Think about it...if they let their home get to the point of having that "rehab look," they are usually motivated to sell. Work out a price that seems fair to both parties, write up a contract, get a 60+ day close, and only put a very small ($10) deposit down. Remember: They are the motivated ones.

Immediately start advertising the property—Place an ad in the local paper: "Handyman Special, Cheap, Cash. 555-555-5555." You will find that you'll get a lot of calls but, unfortunately, not all of them will be any good. You should be looking for handymen, rehabbers, contractors, and other investors.

Once someone shows interest, **negotiate** a price ($5,000–$10,000 above your set price with the seller). Also make sure that you put the closing costs in the buyer's (handyman's, investor's, etc.) contract.

Close and collect the check!—To set up the closing, call a few local title companies in the phone book and ask them if they will do a simultaneous close (two contracts closing at the same time). This can be done with the original seller and the new investor in two separate rooms. Close with your buyer first then with the homeowner. You get your check that same day! (Depending on the state you live in, you'll want to get details and the thumbs-up from your real estate attorney on simultaneous closings.)

As you can see, with wholesale deals you can make great money. Think about it…what if you only did one a month? Would an extra $5,000 to $10,000 per month help you out at all?!

Foreclosures

I can't say enough about foreclosure opportunities earning income for the investor. Investing in foreclosures is one of the best ways of buying real estate at below-market or wholesale prices—and it's one business that flourishes in a slumping economy. Although the housing market is showing signs of cooling, analysts at RealtyTrac say that the bulk of foreclosure sales are still to come in 2007 and 2008 as 323,102 properties become available to buy and sell—at a significant profit.

Foreclosure numbers for the first part of 2006 showed the nationwide average increasing for the fourth consecutive quarter—with an incredible 78% jump over last year and no end in sight. That means that while the supply seems almost unlimited, the only thing greater is Americans' unending and enduring passion to own a home. And with 300,000,000 Americans and more immigrants arriving here each day from all over the world, you better believe that the demand for housing or renting is in no way hurting.

There is no bad time to invest in foreclosures. As experts at *Investors.com* point out, "Buying foreclosures has made a lot of people rich, in good Real Estate markets and bad." But the best time to invest is after you've learned the essentials.

Foreclosing is the process by which a bank or lending institution assumes the title on a property because the purchaser failed to make required payments—and with bad budgeting, shortsighted overspending and families strapped to their financial limits, it's no surprise that the number of home foreclosures is on the rise every day. The buyer should always beware of "100% financing"—the economic impossibility of purchasing property with absolutely no money down. People desperate to own their own home (or strict believers in instant gratification) often make the mistake of committing to this type of arrangement without realizing that they will be living on the financial edge where only one unexpected bill or unforeseen medical expense will push them over. Yet so many Americans still take this plunge.

Another factor contributing to the sharp rise in foreclosures is overborrowing for refinancing. Some lenders are offering loans in excess of 110%, tempting homeowners to pull all of the equity out of their houses for immediate cash to cover other expenses. (Equity is the difference between the current market value of your home and the amount you still owe on the mortgage; it's the amount you would receive after selling the property and paying off the mortgage.) In theory, borrowing in excess of your home's current value is simply a way of tapping into future equity. In reality, it's gambling with your future.

There are other possible reasons for foreclosure: The owner may fail to meet other loan requirements such as insurance coverage. Absentee owners may fail to effectively manage the property, resulting in serious or irreversible maintenance problems that cost more than the property is worth. What does all this have to do with you investing in real estate? Simple. Before you attempt to take over any properties, find out the reason for foreclosure. Potential problems with the property will cost you money and certain foreclosure procedures may cost you time.

In a mortgage state, property owners who have defaulted on a mortgage must go to court themselves to seek legal remedies, including a judicial foreclosure. This process can take anywhere from three months to a year. In a deed of trust state, real estate purchases include a provision that the title to a property is held in trust until the mortgage is paid. In that case, it is the job of the trustee (the individual who acts on behalf of the trust) to foreclose and, usually, to sell the property as soon as possible. This nonjudicial process can be concluded in as little as two to three months.

For real estate investors, foreclosures are not hard to find. They are a matter of public record and must be filed with the county or state recorder with notices printed in the local newspaper. There are also services you can subscribe to that provide information on foreclosures through daily or weekly e-mails (one free service is *www.foreclosuresus.com.*)

In addition to the availability and the ease of finding foreclosures, there are numerous steps during the process that can lead to substantial payoffs before foreclosing even begins. Buying directly from the owners saves you money and saves everybody time, compared to a drawn-out auction or full foreclosure proceedings. It also ensures discretion for the owners, many of whom would rather take less money to save some embarrassment.

So how do you find out about impending fore-closures before the general public? With a little extra effort. Besides on-line sites (such as *www.ipreforeclosures.com*), you can visit County Recorder Offices, the local government branches that keep records of preforeclosure notices sent to owners. Granted, this isn't the most glamorous way to spend an afternoon, but it could save you thousands of dollars.

Since foreclosures are emotionally charged events, dealing directly with the lending institu-tion instead of the owner may be beneficial to all involved. When a lender holds the title to a house, they may be inclined to negotiate a below-market deal to get themselves out from under any expenses associated with correcting code violations or building maintenance. With the right price, you can still come out on top after taking care of these problems.

Banks often have Real Estate Owned listings, which specialize in local preforeclosure properties put up for sale by the bank as the main lender; these "short sale" transactions are done exclusively with the bank and exclusively in cash. Banks' Loan Loss Mitigation Departments work with owners facing foreclosure to help them sell the property—and pay off their outstanding debts—as soon as possible; staff should be able to direct you to some prime property before it goes public. Other lending institutions and real estate agents usually have similar information about preforeclosure sales.

Doing a little homework doesn't hurt either. You can check newspapers for House Rentals or For Sale by Owner ads, which are often the last resort of cash-strapped homeowners. In addition, newspapers' public notices of divorce proceedings, bankruptcy and probate filings can clue you in to properties that may be moments away from foreclosure (it's best to contact the parties involved by mail with a politely worded inquiry about purchasing their property). Finally, you can take out your own ad in the local news-paper of a particular neighborhood stating that you buy preforeclosure property directly—and discreetly— from owners. Keep in mind that some areas with the highest foreclosure rates have below-average unemployment and above-average per capita, but because of high home prices in these desirable locations, owners are stretched to their final limits. These are the types of neighborhoods you should target.

The actual foreclosure is a step-by-step process, leaving many opportunities for the investor to make an offer at the most beneficial moment. In real estate, location may be every-thing…but in investment, it's all about timing!

Preforeclosure: A foreclosure always begins with a written notice from a bank or lender to the property owner informing them that a payment has been missed or other requirements are not being met. This preforeclosure period presents an excellent buying opportunity. Property owners on the verge of imminent eviction are almost always in need of immediate cash for moving and relocation costs. They will often settle for less money sooner rather than more money later. Plus they're usually anxious to take advantage of any opportunity that will offer them the chance to preserve their credit status to buy another home in the future. This preforeclosure period can allow you to purchase the property at well below market value before the formal foreclosure even begins.

Besides saving yourself money, preforeclosure deals help families who need this opportunity to start over. In California alone, 75% of homeowners who took advantage of this option were able to maintain their credit plus pay off existing loans. Experts at Default Research describe preforeclosures as an excellent way "for both parties to benefit. Investors get property at a lower price and families get out of trouble." When I think of all the heartache and grief that preforeclosure saves families from, I'm glad that my investment opportunity also gives others a second chance.

Notice of Default: If the owner does not respond to written letters of late payments, the next step is a notice of formal legal action, known as a Notice of Default. At this point, the owner is already facing late charges, penalties and other fees that may double the amount of the monthly mortgage payment. This is a good time for the investor to make a move. Offer to buy the property at a discount and pay off the remaining mortgage, leaving the owners with only a record of slow payment on their credit reports, which sure beats a foreclosure.

Foreclosure Sale: In a mortgage state, if the owner does not respond to notices of payments due, the lending institution automatically wins a judgment by default. They can advertise the property for four to six weeks, then, if the owner doesn't come up with the money during that time, put it up for sale to the general public. They'll be eager to recoup their losses, so you should be ready to make an offer, having already checked out and assessed the property thoroughly during the presale period.

In a deed of trust state, a trustee arranges for sale of the property if payments aren't made. That means a sheriff's or public auction is usually held at some place, such as the local courthouse, and is advertised in newspapers as a Trustee's Sale. Before you bid, find out everything there is to know about the property. You may discover unrecorded tax liens or physical faults that make it not worth bidding ten bucks on. But if the property is particularly desirable, there are usually lots of interested (and often low-bidding) buyers, so go to the auction with sufficient financial backing and be prepared to raise the stakes if you're sure that this particular investment can turn a profit.

Redemption Period: Many states still offer the original owners an opportunity to reclaim the property even after the sale, provided they can pay the full amount owed, including late charges, legal fees, penalties, etc. That usually isn't the case, but this redemption period offers the smart investor a chance to make the owners a last-minute offer on the deed, regardless of the outcome of the sale. If the owner agrees to your price (particularly if you come with cash in hand), you obtain the redemption rights and can claim the property during this period. This private offer is a particularly savvy strategy if you missed the auction or if public bidding was threatening to drive the property price too high. If you already succeeded in purchasing a property at auction, keep in mind that the original owner can still reclaim the property, so put off any major renovations until after this redemption period has expired.

A recent RealtyTrac survey shows that one in every 358 American houses is in the process of foreclosure at this very moment, especially in targetable places like Indianapolis, Miami, Atlanta, Dallas, Denver, Las Vegas and parts of California. Face it: Foreclosures are a fact of life now all over the country. Some may argue that this signals the end of the American Dream. But for the investor, and quite often the seller, it represents a land of opportunity.

Rehabbing

Forget the Betty Ford Clinic. This kind of rehabbing is a way of refurbishing real estate to make it worth more than what you bought it for. If you've ever seen the TV show Flip This House, you know there are huge profits to be made. Unfortunately, a nice coat of paint won't cut it. We're talking some serious elbow grease.

The first thing to look for when deciding to undertake this type of investment is the building's structure. If there are cracks in the foundation or other serious structural damage, it could get expensive and make this property a losing proposition. Other areas to pay attention to are the roof, plumbing and electricity, since problems in any of these will also add up.

Once you determine that the real estate is worth refurbishing, plan to put a lot of time and effort into it if you're doing it yourself. I mean a lot, like an additional part-time job. The best bet for renovation is to modernize an old bathroom; the return on the money invested in that alone is 102%. Kitchens and windows come next. For the repair-challenged, it may actually be more cost effective to hire someone to do the major work; you can always add the finishing touches like paint and landscaping.

Don't show a refurbished house until it is at least 95% complete since the sight of hanging wires and half-finished ceilings will usually cause the potential buyer to drop the price and duck for cover.

The advantage to rehabbing real estate is that a good fixer-upper can net you $40,000 to $60,000 in earned income—and many investors fit four or more into one year, a sum that easily eclipses many white-collar salaries.

Keep in mind that investing in real estate isn't something you should just do as a fast fix for cash. It's more than that: It's about providing homes for families, adding something to a community, building up your own character. Investors who only have an eye on making a quick buck are the ones who end up making mistakes. If you don't love it, don't do it. Yes, America is the land of opportunity. But don't forget that part about the pursuit of happiness.

Losing My Reality and Finding My Obligation

Although my marketing firm was doing well, I still felt like there was something missing. I had just turned 21, was living in a house that I owned and had recently ended my second engagement to yet another man who wasn't motivated in the slightest.

At this point, my life revolved solely around me and my immediate wants. And I figured why not? I was making fantastic money...when I fell into the trap of Too Much Stuff. Like most people my age and the majority of Americans (even those who can't afford it), I felt like I needed to show my status with a fancy car, expensive clothes, a top-of-the-line cell phone and anything else that the media makes it clear we have to have to be considered "somebody" in society. We fall into a cycle where our income goes right out the window.

Luckily, it got old fast. Growing up the way I did, I realized that stuff is just that—stuff. What you own certainly doesn't determine who you are. My family lived for a while in Mexico when I was 14 and, let me tell you, if you have never been out of the U.S., take my advice and book the next flight out. It will change your life and open your eyes. I've traveled all over America—from Alaska to Hawaii, California to the Carolinas—and I don't care what part of the country you're from or what you think your excuses are. If you live in the U.S., you are blessed beyond belief. We have opportunities here that people in other parts of the world couldn't even imagine. You could start your own business, own your own home, save for your future—yet so many of us waste it all on stupid stuff! You think you need a cell phone that plays music, takes pictures and shows videos? Isn't that what the iPod, digital camera and DVD player you already own do?

In Mexico, where my family spent over a year, the per capita income is only $9,000 a year and 8% of the children are suffering from malnutrition. In Africa, the conditions are even worse. The majority of South African nations have a less than $250 per capita income. Americans would easily blow that in one afternoon on a pair of couture shoes that are too uncomfortable to walk in (so add cab fare to the equation) or a pair of baseball tickets to a game that we could otherwise watch on one of the three TV sets in our home.

Can you imagine what people from other countries would do with the opportunities we have? They sure wouldn't throw it all away on things that get thrown away in just a few years' time. Yet, here we are, living in the richest nation on earth, and instead of leading comfortable lives we're struggling to keep our heads above water financially!

Having almost unlimited opportunities doesn't give us, as Americans, a license to spend, spend, spend. In fact, it's quite the opposite. We have an obligation to do something with those opportunities and to make something of ourselves.

It occurred to me when I was 19, sitting at the kitchen table in my first apartment, writing out the bills for all the senseless stuff I bought, that I had a responsibility to make the most of the opportunities around me by investing in them. And it's still my belief that every American should shut up with the excuses and the whiny attitudes and stop spending each paycheck on frivolous things that you think you can't live without. Unless it's food, air or shelter, you can live without it. Put that money in stocks, property or a savings account instead.

You have no excuse not to retire rich. You have no excuse not to give to your favorite charity. And you have no excuse to be depressed about your life or your economic situation. You have it easy compared to people in other countries. You have opportunities. What you don't have is the luxury of any more excuses.

Step #3: How many times have you heard someone say, "There just aren't any opportunities out there anymore"? Well, I'm proof of the contrary. In fact, by creating so many opportunities of earned income for myself, I have made the mistake of running in a million different directions at once, only to have them all fall through my fingertips.

Don't do what I did. Define what you want, even if you change your mind later. It's better to set your energy on achieving a few specific goals than trying to make a whole bunch of things work at once. But remember: Relying on a nine-to-five job alone just isn't feasible anymore in these troubled financial times. An additional source of earned income has become a modern necessity.

CHAPTER FOUR

MAKE YOUR MONEY MULTI-TASK

The Pros of Passive Income

While there are a lot of advantages to additional earned income, there is an obvious pro to passive income—namely, putting your money to work for you. Passive income is composed of profits from rental properties or other investment enterprises, including on-line ventures, that do not require your active involvement. In other words, you can create streams of income while you're busy enjoying time with your family, relaxing on vacation or simply sitting on your butt. There are thousands of true stories about real people who made it rich, freed themselves from their nine-to-fives and are now living the lives they want, all because they learned to effectively earn passive income. And what could be better than that?

First of all, you should know that you are responsible for your own passive income. The time, energy and effort you put into creating it will pay off, while the longer you continue to do absolutely nothing outside of your normal source of income is both wasted time and wasted potential, not to mention profits lost while you're earning money for someone else. Can you really afford to be that uninterested in making your own money?

While salaries, job markets and benefits are decreasing, the average work life is increasing. Passive income could mean the difference between being in the office well into your 60s or enjoying an early and relaxing retirement. Why depend on $1,000 a month (if that much!) from Social Security that may not even be around much longer when, in as little as five years, you could get $10,000 a month in passive income and officially withdraw from the rat race?

You're probably wondering why it's so important to start thinking about passive income now. Because the average American family is barely surviving paycheck-to-paycheck! Consider this: Parents have eighteen years to save for their children's college fund. But in that amount of time, they can hardly save up even a fraction of tuition costs while still covering daily living expenses. So when high school comes to an end and any chance to save for college is officially over, the family goes into debt the day their pride and joy moves into the dorm room. In fact, the average American family has only enough savings to last through one or two lost paychecks *(www.tcf.org)*. The majority of us are financial wrecks waiting to happen.

Most jobs require trading time for money. In other words, you have an eight- to ten-hour workday in which to earn income, bartering your labor for pay. In order to increase your salary, you'd need to increase the hours you devote to your job. But a lot of companies don't offer paid overtime and, ask yourself, do you really want your only chance to see Hawaii to be when you look at the poster taped longingly to your cubicle wall? Don't be dependent on your boss handing you a paycheck each week. What happens when that comes to an end one day due to outsourcing, layoffs, disability or company closures? That's the future that a lot of us are facing. But now's the time to take control and do something to ensure it doesn't become your reality. Passive income gives you the chance to take an active role in determining your own financial destiny.

Let me put it this way: With all the ways to earn passive income out there, it's nobody's fault but your own if you don't act on them immediately. Unless, of course, you like being broke...

Multiple Streams of Income

Having multiple streams of income isn't as intimidating as it sounds. After all, aren't we all juggling a lot of things as it is? A social life and a work life. A nine-to-five job and some part-time work you take on to make ends meet. Family and a career. A mortgage and monthly bills. While the word "multiple" may sound hard to manage, multiple income actually frees up your time while setting you on your way toward financial freedom.

Our Wisconsin home.

The barn.

The outhouse.

Me (12 years old) and my sister Mallory.

My mom and my sister Tori.

My grandpa and me in Wisconsin.

My brother Sean and our chicken.

Me (13 years old), Sean, and my goat Buddy.

Monterrey, Mexico—At the orphanage with Mallory, Sean and Tori, washing clothes.

Fourteen years old with my friend Melinda.

Hanging clothes in Monterrey.

Robert Kiyosaki (author of
"Rich Dad Poor Dad") and
Me."

Me with Donald Trump.

Me with Regis Philbin.

One of the great things about passive income is that it can make you feel like you're part of a double-income couple, even if you haven't been on a date in years due to the hectic work schedule you've been juggling up to now. It makes it possible for you to bring in more money despite the physical impossibility of being in two offices at the same time. And the most convenient part is that you can earn passive income part-time in addition to a regular job, or full-time as a primary venture. Either way, generating various sources of income is not just an option anymore; it's a necessity. Think of it not just as making your money work, but making it multi-task, the same way we all do in our daily lives.

Get 'Net Working

Opportunities for passive income have never been as plentiful as they are today, thanks to the Internet. People are actually making a living buying items and reselling them in much larger markets such as *Craigslist* and *eBay*. Anyone with a special skill or something unique to say can write on-line articles or set up websites that generate passive income for years to come.

There are plenty of e-businesses that can be built which, over time, are able to run automatically while earning you continual income. They are so easy to get started that you can even do them part-time while working at your main business, pursuing other interests or actually enjoying an abundance of free time. One such example is an affiliate program that reroutes website visitors to a company's product, providing you with referral commission for each on-line sale that company makes. Imagine: You never have to handle the merchandise, warehouse it or deal with customers. All you do is set up a site and reap the rewards. It's like having Levi's pay you advertising costs for wearing a pair of their jeans!

If you have a site that attracts hundreds of visitors each day (and it's amazing how many do…a site in Japan got something like a billion hits a day just for streaming video of some kittens at play), you can sell banner or link spaces to companies for monthly fees. Often, the more specialized or eclectic your site, the more eager companies with a common link will be to advertise on your space. Interested in motorcycle repair? So is BMW. At least, they're interested in the people who visit your site and will happily

pay you for advertising space to promote their own line of motorcycles to your visitors.

How do you get started? Register a cheap domain name with a service such as *www.godaddy.com*. If necessary, hire a professional to give your webpages an attractive, uncluttered appearance that will appeal to both advertisers and visitors. Keep track of how many hits you get and update your site often to keep visitors' interest strong.

In addition, you can also bring highly-targeted traffic to your website by buying pay-per-click *AdWords* that are displayed next to relevant searches (as "sponsored sites") or by investing in Search Engine Optimization that places your webpage among the top ten most-searched results for a given keyword or phrase. The more hits you have, the more advertisers will be interested in your site because it means more hits for them—then the more potential you have for passive income to really start rolling in.

One side note here: The term "passive" income isn't entirely accurate. In addition to your initial investment, planning and effort, be prepared to perform periodic upkeep to ensure that your site is up-to-date so the cash flow doesn't get clogged. In other words, earning passive income takes an active imagination and an occasional hands-on approach on your part.

An Interesting Investment

The world is full of opportunities to create passive income—and I don't just mean the World Wide Web. All it takes is some ingenuity and initiative, traits this nation was founded on. In fact, every American who is able to should make some investment in a source of passive income—and at the age of 13, I made mine.

After a few years of selling chicken eggs and porcupine quills, I had managed to save a startling $25. Adding that to the $5 I had gotten from my grandpa, I felt rich! But now what? Would I buy the Barbie I wanted, keep myself in candy for a year, splurge on a new outfit?

I couldn't decide. But the one thing I was certain of was that after I bought whatever it was, the money would be gone and I would have to start saving all over again. So I decided to spend the money on something that could get me my money back. Forget pork belly trading—I went whole hog and invested in a piglet.

I attended an auction with my parents who helped me bid on a good-looking piglet who I bought and brought home with me for $25. I fed her and took care of her, looking after my investment until the end of summer when I was ready to sell. A farmer bought her for $75, which means I made an extra $50! And from that moment on, I knew I was an investor.

Many years later, when people at my seminars ask me about that piglet, I tell them that I "sau-sage potential in her" (get it?…"saw such potential")! But, seriously, it occurred to me that that first investment taught me a very valuable financial lesson in later years: Taking the time to invest in something that will produce a profit is more important than wasting money on something you feel social pressure to own immediately.

I applied that very same concept to buying real estate, which is one of the best income-producing investments you can make. I rented out housing over the years before selling at a nice profit, so not only did ownership of the property give me equity but the rent brought in continuous revenue. In that way, I didn't just work for my investments—my investments worked for me and for my future wealth.

Real Estate—The Real Deal for Revenue

According to Financial Web, about 98% of the world's millionaires made their fortunes from investing in real estate. That's because recurring revenue from rental property is often one of the best sources of passive income. From these kinds of investments, even average Americans can earn more, work less and be able to afford a comfortable retirement in a shorter amount of time. In a world where we have multiple credit cards, multiple outstanding debts, multiple-car families and a myriad of ways to spend our money, doesn't it make sense to generate multiple streams of income?

I moved out of my parents' home on almost the exact day I turned 18 and, like so many other young adults, entered the world of renting. For $650 a month, I lived in a one-bedroom apartment with a small bathroom where it felt like I was flushing my rent money down the toilet for a year! I finally couldn't take throwing my money away like that and decided to buy a house. Well, I didn't just wake up one day and decide that. I actually called a real estate company and asked them if they knew of any homes in the area for rent. Looking back, they probably considered my call the stupidest they had received in a while, but they told me about some houses for sale instead and I bought the first one I saw.

That probably wasn't the smartest move either, but it ended up working out pretty well. A month after buying the house, I took $25,000 out of its equity and invested that in tax liens. From then on, I was hooked.

My tax liens earned incredible interest! It's different in every state, but mine made 13% (we'll talk more about Tax Liens in Chapter 5). I was actually making money...rather, my money was making me money. Even better, my money was in multiple investments all working toward the same goal of giving me financial freedom.

I lived in that first house for a couple of years before taking more money out and reinvesting it. Then I rented it out for passive income. But the greatest part about the whole situation was that I was writing off the interest on my mortgage payment. For that reason alone, if you don't have real estate you need to get some because tax deductions ROCK. With all the deductions and tax rebates, you practically live for free! Ok, maybe not for *free,* but every dollar of interest you pay is a dollar you wont have to give to Uncle Sam!

Let's look at this example from interest.com:
    With a $100,000 30-year mortgage at 8%, the monthly payment on that loan would start at $734, adding up to $8,808 a year. Of that, $7,970 is considered interest. So by the end of

that first year, you may have only reduced the size of your loan by $838—but you gave yourself an awesome tax write-off of $7,970!

I just sold that first house on a lease option for $250,000—I had originally bought it for $185,000. So, overall, it has made me at least $65,000, not counting all the tax deductions, rental income and lease option payments. I'd say it was more than a valuable investment—it was an invaluable learning experience.

Mobile Homes

While mobile phones are becoming smaller and easier to lose, mobile homes are part of a growing market and are easy opportunities for the investor to find. This type of housing is generally inexpensive and doesn't require a lot of upkeep so it's also ideal for multiple purchases. Mobile homes also generate large amounts of passive income from rent. Can you hear me now?

Having more affordable housing makes sense in uncertain economic times and mobile homes make up a large segment of the manufactured housing sector. Though this aspect of the real estate market hasn't had the same overwhelming success as the recent housing boom, it doesn't suffer the same busts either, making it a steady source of money for the smart investor.

According to *Money* magazine, stocks in manufactured housing show a yearly gain of 14%, so you might want to consider buying into one of these publicly traded companies or safely investing in companies that supply manufactured housing building materials. This way, you don't deal directly with the property or the residents. It's hands-free investing! Another possibility is buying shares in a Real Estate Investment Trust (REIT) that specializes in this type of housing. REITs are securities investing in properties or mortgages that typically offer attractive returns. They are sold on the major stock exchanges or purchased through mutual funds and are considered by many experts to be one of the best and most liquid ways of investing in real estate.

Low-Income Housing

Before we get into what investing in low-income housing exactly is, let's be clear about what it is *not*.

Investing in low-income housing does not make you a "slumlord" and the building will not be in the middle of a battlefield. That said, being a landlord is never easy, not for low-, middle- or upper-income properties. Nor is it a fast track to financial freedom since it takes a while to build a cash flow base. But investing in this kind of property *can be* more sensible than constantly buying and selling real estate because it means significant tax incentives put in place to specifically encourage investors to renovate run-down buildings. Scout surrounding neighborhoods and invest in an area where a great need for low-income housing is apparent.

Overall, low-income housing investments ensure a steady passive income every month that will increase dramatically once any debt associated with the property is paid off—and the initial cost is usually far less than for higher-income real estate. Best of all, you'll be maintaining affordable, decent places to live for a whole lot of people, which is worth a lot in itself.

In fact, the government wants to help provide living assistance to lower-income families who make half of the median income. Section 8 housing is a federal program that offers rental subsidies and limits monthly rent for those who qualify. That's great, but how does it help investors, you're wondering? For one thing, it guarantees on-time rent collection to landlords, as well as ensuring long-term tenants and shorter vacancies—which translates into a steady source of income. Consider that your reward for helping to serve public needs.

Multifamily Housing

Apartments and condos generally provide good to excellent appreciation potential and, if managed properly, almost always ensure positive passive cash flow, so what's not to love? Well...for one thing, you're in charge of maintenance. So either dust off your snow shovel or hire an on-site property manager.

Multifamily housing comes in two flavors—four units or fewer and five units or more. Because they are considered by lenders to be residential property, housing with four units or lower usually garners more favorable financing from lenders than that with five or above, which is considered commercial property and requires a 20% down payment on loans. So while in this case, at least, less may really seem to be more, there are creative ways to get around this payment with seller carrybacks, a financial tool similar to promissory notes.

Converting multifamily housing into condos definitely adds property value, but this undertaking may be difficult depending on zoning laws and estimated construction costs. Although buying apartments that have already been converted into condos may seem like an easier solution, it's actually trickier since they are often older buildings in which only cosmetic changes have been made. There's only so much that a new paint job can hide—and prewar plumbing, pre-Internet wiring and paper thin walls are not in that category. Imagine: Someone in Unit A sneezes, the person in Unit B says "Gesundheit" then promptly calls you to complain about the noise!

For higher returns, your best choice is a sound, up-to-date structure where all that is needed is some simple cosmetic changes to allow you to raise both the rent *and* the market value. You may have to pay more for it, but it'll be more than worth it in the end.

Renting Without Residents

Recently, *Money* magazine offered a novel suggestion for keeping passive income flowing into your pockets without the hassles of tenants weighing on your mind. Instead of housing people, simply store their stuff! Like I said before, Americans accumulate a lot of stuff, so storage facilities will always be a lucrative investment. That and waste disposal!

After your initial investment in a storage facility, many of which are often located on the outskirts of town due to their size (meaning lower property prices and more savings for you), you'll need to consider overhead and upkeep. Other than that, the monthly rental fees you collect are almost pure profit since maintenance and any additional employee salary costs are low.

The best part about this whole investment is that, as the owner, you're entitled to any unclaimed belongings left after a certain set time. With all those leftover telescopes and trophy moose heads, think of the killing you could make on eBay alone!

Lease/"Subject To" Options

Short of becoming a squatter, there are two ways of acquiring real estate with nothing down. Sellers may even give you money up front to help finance the purchase of their property.

A lease option puts you in full control of property instantly with the right to purchase it at a later date (you can change your mind if the market cools or you find some fault with the structure). Some sellers prefer this option because they don't give up the title, and many lenders are willing to treat lease options as regular financing deals, which makes it an attractive way to acquire upper-income real estate you may assume to be outside your price range. But you'll need to investigate the sellers carefully since they'll still own the title—a stipulation that makes you subject only to short-term capital gains until you hold the property for a year.

Under a "lease/subject to" agreement, buyers get the deed to a property without a new mortgage but still make payments on the old one. This means the title is in your name, making it easier to get refinancing and long-term gains. Depending on how badly the owners want out (for relocation purposes, divorce, etc.), they may even be willing to pay you to take the title off their hands.

The bad part about this type of arrangement is that you can't change your mind about buying no matter what happens in the market, and you'll be paying premiums on two insurance policies (one for the seller's original lender and one as the new owner). In addition, sellers are less likely to sign over a deed to property with a lot of equity.

However, despite these drawbacks, lease options give you greater leverage when negotiating with the owner—which means a greater chance of getting the real estate you *really* want and renting it out for passive income.

Commercial Real Estate

Commercial real estate (office buildings, strip malls, warehouses) is the realm of knowledgeable investors—not novices. There are considerable long-term benefits to owning commercial property, not the least of which are large amounts of portfolio income and the ability to use some of the space to run your own business rent-free. But while it's important in all types of real estate transactions to do your homework beforehand, in commercial investing, it's absolutely essential.

Deciding where to purchase a piece of commercial property is in itself a time-consuming process that could take months or years of analyzing data. How often does space become available? How much time elapses before it's rented out? What kinds of businesses move in and how long do they tend to stay? None of this information is significant based only on a short-term study.

When small businesses move out of a commercial space, owners are almost always faced with costly renovation and customized remodeling before it can be leased to another tenant. And small businesses tend to move out fast, either outgrowing the space or becoming unable to afford the rent. A general slowdown or upswing in the local economy translates into lots of losses or profits for the owner, so your research has to take geographic growth and trends into account.

Investing in commercial real estate means constantly dealing with change...but it can also mean dealing in *a lot* of dollar bills. Unless you have significant experience in real estate, commercial real estate may not be the best place to start. Get your feet wet, collect your first few checks, do your research then jump in!

Financing Your Dreams

With all the profit to be made in the multiple strategies of real estate investing, you may wonder why everyone isn't involved. Many people simply don't think they have the money to make money.

But there are ways to finance your dreams without shelling out a fortune up front.

One way is seller financing. Not all owners selling their property are out to get their hands on as much money as possible as soon as possible— although that is a popular motive. Some sellers are interested in financing the transaction themselves because of the returns associated with mortgage lending, the significant amount of equity in their property or the shorter time it takes to complete the process personally. None of these are cause for concern for the investor. However, if the seller is anxious to finance the sale because the property wouldn't qualify for a conventional loan, it's best to let this "opportunity" slip through your financially conscious fingers.

In a seller-financed deal, the owner agrees to an amount that will allow the investor to purchase the property directly instead of through a 15- to 30-year mortgage. The benefit for the buyer is obvious; for the seller, payment over time is a smart way to reduce taxable income. Depending on the market and if the property is in less-than-perfect condition, some owners are even willing to negotiate interest fees and flexible payment schedules. But if sellers seem a bit too eager to finance your purchase themselves, it's a strong indication there's something wrong with the property they're trying to unload on you.

A final note of caution: Seller-financed agreements should **not** contain a due-on-sale clause (which lets the lender demand full payment of outstanding loans from you as soon as the property is sold) or a recourse clause (giving the lender the right to foreclose, sell the property, levy a point value against you and pursue your assets in order to cover any outstanding debts). Don't just read the fine print—study it under a microscope.

For What It's Worth

We've all heard that location, location, location are the three most important considerations in buying real estate. If only it were that easy! Property value is actually determined by a lot of other things as well. No matter what a low price you paid for your purchase, it isn't a good investment unless it can show a profit. To help make that happen, keep the following factors in mind:

Desirability—What is the current demand for this kind of property in this area? Even a three-bedroom house with a big backyard may not sell if it isn't in a good school district.

Scarcity—Are there similar, equally desirable properties in the same area? Do they cost less? Are they vacant?

Transferability—How easy is it to transfer ownership? Are there obstacles (land ordinances, lender clauses) that make it more difficult?

Utility—Is the property in the right place to meet needs? For example, would you purchase an office building on a mountaintop because of its spectacular views? Not if you expect to make any money!

Trust me, there are a lot of ways to invest successfully in real estate, even in a cooling market, but each of them requires research, patience and smart choices. Do your homework before buying any sort of property to save yourself a disaster down the road.

If your research provides satisfactory answers to all of the previous questions, then chances are you've found the real deal in real estate investment. Go for it! You can thank me after you've made your first million...

Step #4: Passive income is absolutely essential in this day and age. Almost no one can afford to live a comfortable lifestyle on one source of income anymore. Even families that earn upwards of $200,000 go into debt due to the overwhelming costs of college tuition, mortgage payments, medical bills and retirement—it's a cycle of spending that lasts a lifetime and it's proving almost impossible for most Americans to get ahead that way.

Why depend on what other people feel like paying you when there are so many sources of passive income available? You are the only one who can earn financial freedom and more free time for yourself. Don't expect the higher-ups at your company to do it for you. After all, those things aren't exactly in your boss's best interest!

CHAPTER FIVE

LET YOUR PORTFOLIO CARRY YOU

An Economic Essential

Here's what you need to know about portfolio income: You cannot live without it. No matter how young you are, you have to think about getting a portfolio started soon...and I mean YESTERDAY!

Portfolio income is the money you earn from investments (pension plans, dividends from stocks, interest from bonds, royalties, real estate, etc.). Like passive income, portfolio income gives investors a chance to earn money without directly working for it. It's like found money, only better, because it appreciates while you leave it alone. Think of it like this: You reach into the pocket of your winter coat and discover that twenty-dollar bill you left there last year and forgot all about. Except somehow it turned into a fifty!

An Imperfect Storm

"Federal Reserve Chairman Ben Bernanke warned that the recent improvement in the U.S. budget deficit is simply 'the calm before the storm.'"

Brian Blackstone/Henry J. Pulizzi, Jan. 18, 2007

Now, I know a lot of you don't want to start planning for retirement just yet but too bad! If you're old enough to have started working and making an income, you're old enough to think about how that money's going to help you in the long run. It's never too early to start making smart decisions, especially ones that benefit you later in life. Retirement may seem like a long time away but if you have the right amount of passive income, you'll be able to retire a lot sooner (and a lot richer) than you think!

Another Day, Another Dollar

The retirement strategy of most Americans can be summed up in a few lines of Merle Travis' lyrics:

> *You load sixteen tons and what do you get?*
> *Another day older and deeper in debt.*
> *Saint Peter, don't you call me 'cause I can't go*
> *I owe my soul to the company store.*

Let's just say it's not a happy song, nor was it a good way to ever come out ahead financially in your lifetime. But it gets worse. At the time the song "Sixteen Tons" was released in 1947, forty-two workers were paying into Social Security for every one recipient. Nowadays, that number has dropped to three (Social Security Administration, Trust Fund Report). So not only is our generation "deeper in debt" than Merle's was, we won't have the same security of a government funds program when we retire.

On top of all that, Americans don't owe just "the company store" anymore—we owe the department store, electronics store, credit card company, utilities companies, car lease dealership and every corner bodega in between! Our debt is due to our own personal spending. So I say stop relying on the government, your company or anyone else to support you and start building a portfolio and private savings that will assure you an independent future.

According to the Office of Research and Economic Analysis, Social Security payments will replace only 16% of the income for a couple earn-

Social Insecurity

"According to Federal Reserve Chairman Ben Bernanke, Social Security is on schedule to go bankrupt by 2040!"

Blackstone/Pulizzi

ing $50,000–$100,000. So, at best, they'd have their company's pension plan to survive on. But most companies don't offer pension plans anymore and many workers in the steel, airline, automotive and textile industries have had their pensions cancelled or drastically reduced. That's why having continual portfolio income is an absolute must!

One Leg to Stand On

Retirement income is sometimes called the three-legged stool (Social Security, pensions, private savings). The problem is that, for most Americans, that stool is too wobbly to depend on. Try sitting on it and you'll fall flat on your face, financially speaking.

Social Security looks like it'll be dried up by the time most of my generation retires (if they're ever able to retire on one source of income) and full pension plans offered by companies are becoming a thing of the past (according to the

Baby Boomers Go Bust!

"Federal Reserve Chairman Ben Bernanke warned of a 'vicious cycle' as the roughly 80 million Baby Boomers start retiring and drawing Social Security and Medicare benefits. That spending will significantly widen the budget deficit, leading to higher debt payments."

Blackstone/Pulizzi

AFL-CIO, less than 37% of workers today will receive traditional pensions). In a lot of cases, you can kiss that pension goodbye! That leaves only one leg to rely on: private savings. So, once again, the responsibility for your future is shifted onto you.

Of course, everybody knows, at least in theory, that they should have "something" put away for retirement. But how much is enough? Some experts say that 75% to 80% of your yearly working income should cover a year of retirement.

Generation Debt

"Higher entitlement spending could cripple the U.S. economy if action isn't taken soon in reforming programs like Social Security and Medicare. 'The U.S. economy could be seriously weakened, with future generations bearing much of the cost,' the Federal Reserve Chairman said."

Blackstone/Pulizzi

But the majority of Americans (nine out of ten) don't have nearly that much saved to stop working at 65! And with rising health costs and increases in daily expenses, even that ideal estimate may not be enough, especially considering that the average life span extends fifteen years after retirement.

Let the cold, hard reality serve as a wake-up call. A poll by the AFL-CIO shows that, in 2006, 27% of retired households had only 50% of their preretirement income saved up...and they're the lucky ones. This means that a staggering number

Total Eclipse of the AARP

"In less than 50 years, the number of retirees will swamp America's ability to pay Social Security benefits. But the fiscal crunch will begin far sooner, as Social Security payments eclipse the revenues that the government will collect within the next decade."

Blackstone/Pulizzi

of us are facing a drastic drop in our standards of living as we get older and many middle-class households will fall below the poverty line. Is that what you've been working your whole life for?

Remember the old concept of retirement: lots of leisure time, leisure suits, golf and gardening? Recently, fewer than half of people 55 or older are expecting to be financially able to lead a leisurely retired life. Even baby boomers' redefinition of retirement as a time for adventure, world travel and things they were too busy to do when they were working seems unlikely even one generation down the road. Though most workers look forward to a better quality of life when they're retired, recent retirees have reported that their standard of living has actually declined.

Traditional workplace benefits are shrinking as fewer employers (just 34% of large firms and only 5% of smaller ones) provide retirement healthcare packages. So workers have to save more in order to make up for this decrease. Well, the truth is that only 50% of all workers participate in some kind of workplace retirement plan, such as a 401(k). That means that fully half the population is facing an uncertain and, frankly, scary financial future.

Goodbye, Golden Years

"Federal economists estimate that if entitlement reform is put off for another 20 years, consumer spending would have to fall by 13.7% to adjust."

Blackstone/Pulizzi

And, even from this small pool of employees who do take advantage by investing in profit sharing and other defined contribution plans offered by their companies, too many of them cash out their 401(k)s early to pay off debt, fend off foreclosure or just to be able to afford normal life expenses like college tuition or their daughter's wedding. Poor financial planning means they cash in their future security— plus they pay a steep fine for early withdrawal and get only a fraction of the potential benefit.

Facing the Future

"Federal Reserve Chairman Ben Bernanke said that economic growth can help mitigate budgetary pressures, but alone can't cure the long-term fiscal problems the U.S. faces."

Blackstone/Pulizzi

Obviously, company pensions aren't going to cut it. And, let's face it: Social Security alone cannot cover all our costs now—and who knows what the future holds? Depending on government programs, company packages, or your winnings from Bingo to take care of you in your old age is deluded thinking. In plain English, it simply ain't gonna happen! So stop holding your breath, hoping things will work out—and start working on your portfolio instead. I mean, if private portfolio income is the only thing that's going to save us in retirement, shouldn't we all be taking it a lot more seriously?

Pension Planning

The first step to putting together a portfolio is to take advantage of any pension plan options that your company may offer. What I mean is: Anyone with a job should already be looking into this! You do a lot for your company—find out what it's willing to do for you.

Before even accepting a position, most of us ask detailed questions about vacation days and lunch breaks but fail to find out anything about company pension plans. It's time to start thinking ahead! Even if your company cafeteria offers the best lunches in the world, you don't want to work there forever, do you?

Here are some of the most common plans available to employees. Ask questions; get informed about which plans, if any, your company offers. Then step away from the coffee maker and go invest!

You can divide these plans into two categories:
- Defined Benefit Plan promises a monthly payment at retirement (generally a flat rate or percentage of recent salary).
- Defined Contribution Plan, such as 401(k) and stock ownership, has the employee, employer or both contributing a percentage of one's

working salary to the employee's account. The employee receives this upon retirement, plus or minus gains or losses due to changing investment values.

Two of the most common examples of defined contribution plans are as follows:

- *Profit Sharing,* in which an allocated amount, determined annually, is invested into an account by several investors. A portion of each contribution, including gains, is later given to each participant.
- *401(k)s,* which, contrary to popular belief, are not a breakfast cereal, a marathon or the newest type of Levi's jeans. They are a type of profit sharing that puts a portion of each employee's salary, before taxes, into the plan. One of the best ways to retire rich is by keeping as much money as possible shielded from taxes, so this built-in tax break is a definite bonus. Besides that, the beautiful part about 401(k)s is that employers also put in a percentage of those contributions or even match them. However, employees manage their own investment options, giving them some control over their future finances. (If your company doesn't offer

a 401(k), QUIT! Just kidding. You can set up an automatic investing program at a fund company or brokerage.)

A study showed that automatic enrollment in contribution plans increased workers' savings from 3.5% to 11.6%. So, essentially, not getting involved in these options is as crazy as refusing an 8% raise! And just think: The sooner you start your portfolio, the sooner you can spend every day at your desk dreaming about how you'll spend your early retirement…and knowing that those dreams will someday come true.

Give Me Equity or Give Me Debt

The next step to getting your portfolio in shape is to start investing privately. You think you need to be a millionaire in order to invest? Wrong! Investing is how many millionaires actually become millionaires in the first place.

Stocks and Bonds
Had enough of retirement and pension plans for now? Let's move on to something that sounds a little

sexier: stocks and bonds. All those Wall Street types talking about "the market." The frenetic energy on the floor of the New York Stock Exchange. Those indecipherable codes in small print in the Financial Times. There's something so very Bond...James Bond...about the whole stocks and bonds thing. But in order to master it, you have to demystify it.

One of the best ways to make the most of the money you have is to invest it in stocks and bonds. A stock (also called a share or an equity) is a security indicating partial ownership in a corporation. If you hold stock in a company, you are considered a shareholder, which means you receive part of the company's earnings (providing there are any) in the form of dividend checks, if the company elects to pay the dividends. Other companies may elect to reinvest all of their earnings in the business. Generally, stocks of companies that pay sizable dividends are defensive (or conservative) and those that reinvest all earnings into the company are called growth stocks.

A bond, in effect, is a loan that you're making to a company or government with the promise that the principal (money borrowed) will be paid back with interest at a specific time in the future (the date of maturity). However, the higher the rate of return, the riskier the investment. That's why corporate bonds, which carry the possibility of bankruptcy before maturity, offer better return rates than treasury bonds, which pay less but are guaranteed by the government and carry almost no risk.

WARNING! One word of caution about so-called penny stocks, which are stocks traded outside of major exchanges (such as the NYSE, NASDAQ or AMEX). There's a reason they're named for our cheapest currency—because they're not worth picking up! Sure, they are low-priced, but they are also extremely speculative since they are often sold by small companies and traded infrequently, which means they're hard to get rid of once you buy them. As the Security and Exchange Commission warns, "Investors in penny stocks should be prepared for the possibility that they may lose their whole investment." And who is ever prepared

for that?! Here's my two cents: Stay
away!

Of course, there are some inherent risks to play-
ing the stock market, too, but there are also
plenty of safe and steady returns to go around.

Mutual Funds

Mutual funds are the most popular form of stock
market investing because they are easy to manage
and you can get your money out as easily as you
put it in.

A mutual fund is an investment from a group of
individuals who have a professional money manager make decisions about what to buy, what to
sell and when to do it. If you decide to put money
into a mutual fund, you become part of that pool
and your resources generally get spread out over a
range of investments. There are many types of
mutual funds with a wide range of strategies,
including growth stocks, value (underpriced)
stocks and those that invest in bonds. In this way,
the risk of loss is significantly lowered because if
one stock goes down, chances are that other
investments will go up. It's a delicate balance, but
remember that the money manager makes the

decisions, does the research and can discern between high- and low-risk returns. All you do is invest, wait and then watch your portfolio income come streaming in!

TIP! Exchange-traded funds (ETFs) are not technically mutual funds but they offer many of the same advantages while trading like a stock. Separately, index funds (like those offered by Vanguard) are low-cost mutual funds that are a fantastic option for those who don't know one mutual fund manager from another (like me!) but want to reap all the benefits of the stock market.

IRAs

If you're Bono, an IRA is the Irish Republican Army. For the rest of us, IRAs (Individual Retirement Accounts) are investment accounts into which individuals can set aside a specified amount of income to invest each year. This is usually deducted from taxable income before taxes are taken out, meaning that IRA contributions and interest are tax-deferred until retirement. And that's great news! Although there aren't many ways that you can avoid the 10% early withdrawal penalty before the age of 59½, there is a mandatory withdrawal age (70½, don't ask me how they arrived at those exact numbers!) at which the money is taken out and taxed.

Want some even better news? Withdrawals from Roth IRAs aren't subject to federal income tax! This is one of the few times that Uncle Sam is willing to give you a break. But there are limits to what he'll let you get away with. Because Roth IRAs are such a good deal, the amount of cash you can contribute is restricted and you won't get the immediate tax deductions, yet they are a much more flexible investment instrument than the traditional IRA.

Annuities

Annuities guarantee that the retirement income you invest will last as long as you live. You're wondering what's the catch, right? There is none, except that once you invest in annuities, don't expect to wake up rich the next morning. Annuities are among the lowest-yielding accounts, meaning that they're ideal for long-term holding. In conjunction with other investment options, annuities (which can be bought from insurance agencies) are a great way to supplement portfolio income in the form of monthly checks—giving you a stream of income you can count on and something more reliable than a Clearinghouse Sweepstakes sitting in your mailbox.

Mixing It Up

You know how everybody seems to have their own advice about dating? Wait three days before calling. It takes half the time of the relationship to get over a breakup. Order the second-most-expensive thing on the menu. It's like we've reduced romance to mathematical formulas!

Well, in the same way, there are all sorts of magic rules about investing. One generally accepted way to figure out the percentage of your long-term savings that should be in stocks is to subtract your age from 120. Don't invest more than 10% of your savings in your own company's stock. And on and on.

But the basic rule that you need to know is that you don't have to sink large sums of money into stocks in order to see a substantial increase in profit. Even moderate investments can lead to nice overall returns in the long run.

My advice? Mix it up. Put some money in safe bets like highly rated corporate bonds and spread some of your savings into a diverse stock portfolio.

The time to invest in riskier (and, hopefully, more financially rewarding) stocks is when you're younger so you still have time to rebound if the market takes a bad turn. Play it safer and invest more in conservative stocks with high dividend payouts and highly rated corporate bonds as you get older.

Keeping Stock

We all have an image of typical stock investors—red-faced, holding a phone up to each ear. In one phone, they're yelling, "BUY!" and in the other, "SELL!" It's a nice ad for ulcer medicine, but this isn't exactly the way it works!

In reality, the best investments are stocks you can hold on to for years to come. By not having to buy and sell every few months, you'll save on taxes and trading costs. Besides, if their records are any indication, the following stocks will weather any temporary dips the market takes. So put away that Pepto!

- Consistent performers, such as utility companies. These are especially good as you get older because they have high dividend yields.
- Suppliers of a large and diverse number of products whose sales don't slow because of a

bad economy (personal grooming giant Procter & Gamble is a good example).
- Technical dominators, which are companies that have cornered a small but essential market or just plain dominate (Microsoft, anyone?).
- Huge banks that survive mergers and are one of the few sectors that prosper during an economic slump as more people take out loans.
- Companies with large oil reserves in North America.

Of course, the market is always going to fluctuate and even stocks that seem like sure bets will periodically plummet. But hold on to these types of stocks for a thirty-year haul and you can expect them to stabilize—then sell sometime after that, when they're at a peak. Better yet, just invest in five or six different mutual funds with different strategies. For example, invest 20% in small cap stocks, 20% in international stocks, 20% in high-dividend stocks, 20% in bonds and 20% in healthcare stock. Each fund has between 100 and 2,000 different stocks. Now that's what I call diversification!

Money magazine profiled one successful stock strategy that was based on long-term holdings.

Brad Hall, who worked for a financial company, knew enough to keep 90% of his 401(k) in stocks that showed a strong and steady history, and the rest in lower-yielding bonds and annuities. His philosophy? "When the market goes down, I don't mind. I know it will go up again."

With that long-term outlook, he was able to make enough money to retire early, after twenty-nine years at his company, and start a business of his own based on his all-consuming passion of restoring and selling high-end classic cars. And what beats a retirement that gives you a second chance to do what you love best? Even with the good income Brad makes from muscle cars, the 80% of his portfolio that he still keeps in stocks is his real vehicle to financial success that will last a lifetime.

Putting Stock in Education

Money also reported that those who attend financial or retirement seminars like the ones I speak at (yes, I know it's a shameless plug, but it's true!) show a subsequent increase of 20% in net worth. Where else can you gain so much simply by sitting in an audience for a couple of hours?

The key to successful investing is educating yourself. Now, I'm not saying you have to pore over the financial pages or become an expert in the NASDAQ (not to be confused with NASCAR). But you will benefit by listening to others who have an extensive financial history and proven success in our chosen areas. What you get is insider information, straight from those who have made it our business to learn everything we could about real estate, investing, generating income and starting small businesses. Seminars like these give you expert knowledge without beginner blunders, and the motivation to go out and do it for yourself.

One of the overriding themes in my seminars is that, when it comes to investing, start early and stick to it. If you start a portfolio at 20 by investing $2,000 a year, at 30 you'll have $34,000. With a 10% annual return, you'll have given yourself a $677,000 sixtieth birthday present. But if you wait even until you're 30 to begin, you'll have to double the amount you invest each year to arrive at the same figure. So I'll say it again: The time to invest in your future is while you're young. There is not one single smarter thing that you will ever do for yourself. Even Albert Einstein said the most important mathematical concept was, in fact, compounding interest. This from the man who came up with the Theory of Relativity! But, I mean, it doesn't take a genius...

A Stream Runs Through It

Since we're talking about multiple streams of income, another way to fatten up your portfolio is through investment properties. Investments in real estate are some of the most lucrative you could ever make. Despite occasional and temporary slumps in the housing and construction sectors, the demand for development continues to be at an all-time high in areas throughout the country. According to the *Seattle Post*, Starbucks franchises are opening nationwide at a rate of four stores per day. Their construction crew must be hypercaffeinated! And in the area around New York City alone, condominiums are going up quicker than cab fares.

With this rapid pace of development, the sooner you strike, the more your investments will be worth.

Lots and Land

Investing in undeveloped land, to avoid the headaches that come with tenants and building maintenance, may be a temptation too strong to pass up. But in this area of real estate investing, more than any other, time really does equal money. Buying at the right time could mean the difference between breaking even and breaking the bank.

If you invest in an area where an economic explosion is imminent, you could cash in greatly—the trick, however, is identifying a lucrative area before everybody else catches on to its potential. There are plenty of opportunities to invest, particularly in areas throughout the country that are undergoing a population boom due to waves of immigration and the relocation of industries.

Before buying, check out all the local factors that can impact land development: environmental regulations, resident petitions against building up the area, and other municipal concerns. These things can leave you holding the deed to a costly piece of property for a very long time. Once they're cleared, you can start looking at empty lots and seeing them filled with dollar signs.

But before you make money, there is some cash that you have to shell out first. You must pay property taxes and liability insurance on land, even if it's only a bunch of weeds and cacti—and those are expenses on property that is not yet producing a penny's worth of portfolio income. So before investing, make sure you can cover these costs.

In addition, land purchases are usually made in cash, which means that you'll be tying up capital. Banks and lending institutions are not especially land purchase-friendly since they consider it speculative investing at best. Expect higher interest and down payments—which you will ultimately make up for in higher returns.

However, do not expect a tax write-off for depreciation; unlike buildings, land value does not depreciate. The good news is that, without depreciation, you can hold on to the property for as long as you'd like to receive your optimum asking price.

The last thing you should know about lots and land? Unfortunately, there's not enough room in this book to tell you about all the investors who made an absolute killing subdividing and selling land to developers and contractors. But you can bet they did plenty of research beforehand to find out what companies were moving into the area, how long they'd likely be holding on to the land before selling, and what improvements had to be made to power lines, sewers and utilities in the area. And they made darn sure they understood local zoning laws and regulations—inside out, upside down and backwards. Remember, with land, you reap what you sow. Don't expect everything to come up roses if you don't put the time in to do the research. Trust me, the money you get out will increase with every minute you put in.

Bottom line? Investing in lots and land means more money out of your pocket up front, but the potential for lots and lots of profit later on.

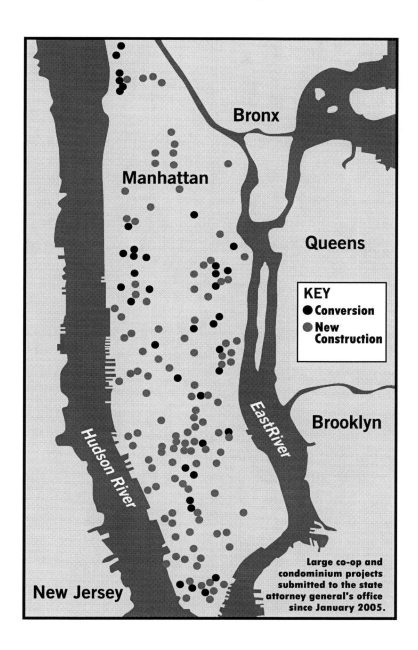

KEY
● Conversion
● New Construction

Bronx

Manhattan

Queens

Brooklyn

East River

Hudson River

New Jersey

Large co-op and condominium projects submitted to the state attorney general's office since January 2005.

Tax Liens

Tax liens present investors with an outstanding opportunity for portfolio income. When an owner fails to pay taxes on a piece of real estate, the local or state government files a lien on their property, allowing banks or creditors to collect the unpaid taxes while setting their own level of interest. The government and the bank are unhappy because they haven't gotten what's owed them and the owner is in a real bind, unable to sell or promise to sell the property before the tax lien is paid off. This is where you step in to help out both sides.

In many cases, the two-year time limit will expire and the county will auction off the property just to raise enough money to cover unpaid taxes and creditor's fees. But, as everyone knows, banks and local governments don't like to wait any longer than they have to to get paid. So, investors get the opportunity to purchase these tax lien certificates, in effect buying themselves the right to collect the taxes and penalties directly from the homeowner—at interest rates set by the state or sometimes the county (an average of 16%). The creditor and county are relieved of that responsibility, plus they receive your payment instead of waiting for the owners to pay off their debts. Plus the owners get to keep their house. It's a win-win for everyone involved.

Your best bets are tax lien certificates against owner-occupied houses primarily because that provides the motivation for owners to pay up or risk foreclosure. Limit yourself to properties you're willing to own since you may end up getting the deed to them—which can turn out to be every investor's dream or an absolute nightmare. That's why it's essential to do an inspection of the property beforehand to ascertain its value—otherwise the tax lien certificate you purchased may end up being worth less than the paper it's printed on. Tax lien auctions held by the county are usually sold by lot number, so without an inspection, you could essentially be buying property sight unseen. The same goes for on-line auction sites.

Finally, there's a chance that the IRS may declare priority to the deed if the owner claims bankruptcy, leaving you with whatever interest you collected (not a bad investment in itself!) but without any property. Not that the IRS would do such a thing...

Don't let these minor points dissuade you. Like any investment, tax liens require a fair amount of research to ensure success. Yet unlike rehabbing or rentals, tax liens don't require a lot of sweat equity.

In fact, they're a hot ticket item right now in the investment world as a great way to get tremendous financial rewards without too much work, freeing you up to pursue other sources of income simultaneously. And that, after all, is the purpose of any good addition to your portfolio.

Step #5: It is never too early to start building your portfolio. In fact, as Social Security shrinks and fewer companies offer pension plans, you are solely responsible for what your quality of life will be like in the future. Investing means the difference between working for the rest of your life to make ends meet, or resting after years of work and making the most out of life.

CHAPTER SIX

STAY TRUE TO YOU

From Real Estate to Reality TV

By 21, I had already gotten a real estate license, was selling and investing in real estate, and was offering investment advice to my clients. What little free time I did have was spent trying to absorb as much information as I could about investing and finance. I had developed a voracious appetite for these subjects and read every relevant book or magazine article and listened to any instructional tape that I could get my hands on—but it still wasn't enough.

I was starting to realize that my small marketing firm, though successful, wasn't giving me enough of a return on all the time I put in and wouldn't bring the level of financial security that I was seeking. For that, I'd have to dive head first into a firsthand education on all possible applications of capital. I needed to learn it from the inside out from someone who looked at business in the same large-scale terms as me. But who?

The answer came after another long day at work, while I was eating a late-night dinner and half-watching, half-listening to the TV. I heard the announcement: "If YOU want to be Donald Trump's apprentice, please apply on-line to…" I couldn't get to my computer fast enough! Here I was, desperately trying to find out everything about building my financial future, and it could all come to me courtesy of NBC.

As it turned out, I had already missed the on-line application deadline, but preliminary interviews were being held nearby for potential contestants. I went for an interview and was called back for several others before finally hearing that I had been selected among fifty finalists to fly to Los Angeles…for even more exciting interviews!

But all this back and forth didn't bother me. I was too busy being ecstatic over this opportunity to learn all about business techniques and investment strategies from one of the financial field's most high-profile players. I got to L.A. and immediately underwent a week of grueling tests—IQ, psychological, medical, you name it. After more intense and personal questioning from the producers, I was finally called up to a presidential suite where Executive Producer Mark Burnett told me that I was the youngest of the 16 selected from over 250,000 applicants to appear on the first season of *The Apprentice*.

My life was never going to be the same again. And I mean that…starting with the fact that I'd have to close down the marketing firm, my main source of income, for a few months to appear on the show—without telling my employees or clients why. I was contractually bound not to discuss my participation on the reality program with more than five friends or family members, who were also signed to secrecy. And if I had expected any support from them for what I was doing, I was dead wrong.

In fact, my parents were so set against the idea that they wouldn't offer me any help at all. So, a few weeks later, I found myself having to hire someone to watch my house and drive me to the airport...alone.

An Apprehensive Apprentice

As soon as I arrived in New York, I began to wonder if this was such a smart decision after all. The truth is, I was starting to lose focus and felt like I was moving even further away from my goals. But pretty soon there wasn't enough time to wonder much about anything. Microphones were strapped to me 24/7 and cameras followed my every move.

The teams of Apprentices took orders from Mr. Trump and were assigned competitive tasks, most of which seemed pretty silly to me. I mean, if I had hoped to find out all about earning and investing fortunes, I sure wasn't going to accomplish that by selling lemonade on the streets of New York City!

By the time it dawned on me that the only thing the show had to offer was entertainment value for the viewing audience—not educational value for the actual participants—it was already too late. I had successfully completed all of the assigned tasks so far only to be fired on the sixth episode.

In the world of reality television, firing someone is as simple as editing videotape and leaving the unwanted scraps on the cutting room floor until there's nothing left of that person. I lost. And that's exactly how this whole experience left me feeling—completely lost.

Derailed

I was back on a plane, sitting in coach and coming home to nothing. As usual, the scratch pad in front of me was filled with all my thoughts, concerns and goals. But inside I felt empty. There I was, the same age as most college seniors and already heading my own marketing firm—and still I felt like a failure. I wondered how temporarily closing down my business would wind up affecting it. I also wondered if I even wanted it anymore. The answer was: I didn't know what I wanted.

Since my parents had begged me not to go on the show, I expected a few "I told you so's" when I called to let them know I was back. Without the hype of going out every night, cameras, constant attention and people to talk to, I felt there was nobody on my side cheering me on and my depression was elevated in those first few weeks home. All of us cast members still had to remain silent about where we were for the last two months, so not only could I not explain where I had been, I didn't even know where I was going and who I was anymore.

I made the conscious decision to put off acknowledging how lost I felt because it was so much easier to just let myself be defined by the show. As I watched in horror every week, I realized that this reality program shaped me into a character I couldn't even recognize. Yes, it looked just like me. But my character was a creation of the editing process, which could make each of us appear to the public any way the producers wanted us to.

As I fought against that image of me on the screen every week, making excuses for myself, I also embraced the status that the show gave me. I obsessed over every bit of media attention, which was a form of validation after I had felt so discarded. Even my parents seemed to change their minds about me and my newfound fame, holding parties at their house every week with their friends—and I was the guest of honor. Relatives who never even acknowledged my birthday suddenly called all the time and my friends wanted to hang out constantly and introduce me to people they knew. I got so many offers from different companies that I was pursuing twenty-five options at once.

But things got worse as the show aired each week. Although no one else knew the outcome yet, I braced myself for the inevitable. In the meantime, people took my picture everywhere I went. I was constantly doing interviews—The *Today Show*, CNBC, Fox News, E!—and flying out to L.A. or New York for parties, so I still didn't have time to reopen my business and I still didn't have an income. What I had instead were fans, stalkers and crazy boyfriends.

"YOU'RE FIRED!"

Everyone treated me like a rich rock star. They really couldn't get enough. I, on the other hand, was miserable. I put on weight, then developed an eating disorder and even contemplated suicide. Then *Playboy* called and I actually thought about posing since I could seriously use the money.

The very next week I was fired in front of the entire nation. And as I watched the disappointment on my friends' and family's faces as they sat around the television set, I knew the party was over. I was yesterday's news just like that. No more jet-setting, no more calls from my relatives, no more popularity. My world had ended once again.

It's funny how fast people forget about you but at the same time it really is a blessing. Being fired from the show gave me a chance to step back from the frenzy and just think. Now that the on-screen image that had defined me was dead, what in the hell was left of me? I had no idea how to answer that so I still went around trying to be "that girl from *The Apprentice*" and it worked for a while until I finally realized, as my bank account and self-esteem were suffering, that that wasn't who I wanted to be.

By this point I had gotten so far off track that I wasn't sure if I could find my way back.

Things were honestly getting so far out of my control until I just forced myself to STOP and take some time to reevaluate my goals and what I wanted out of life—my life, my reality. It would mean working harder than I ever had to get to where I wanted to go now.

Sure, I was on TV. But I was completely out of focus.

Working My Way Back Up

I'm going to tell you something that you really might not want to hear and may even sound a little mean but...I don't care where you are today. Because guess what? IT DOESN'T MATTER! I can sincerely say (and I'm not trying to be egotistical) that I've pulled myself up by my bootstraps on two separate, very different occasions and I'll tell you that it is incredible what you can bounce back from if you just listen to yourself and believe in your dreams. That is exactly what I finally did after my experience on *The Apprentice*. I listened to my own dreams and goals, and that is when I realized what I wanted from my life and began focusing on it to make it my reality. I tuned out what my parents wished for, what the producers felt and the greedy desires of other companies. I just listened to me and kept on listening because your own inner voice doesn't steer you wrong.

Once I started to stay true to myself and work toward what I wanted, I was able to come so far in such a short period of time. My passions have always stayed pretty much the same—only my priorities have changed in that I've stopped seeking other people's approval. Along with this personal growth, my expectations, goals and accomplishments have grown bigger now than ever.

Step #6: Working your butt off and having a belief in yourself, your product and your goals are the basic essentials you need to succeed. They are the things that should remain constant, despite ever-changing markets, an unstable economy, booms and busts. The willingness to give it your all is often the deciding factor between failure and success, so don't let a few setbacks stop you.

And, no matter what, never stop listening to the little voice inside yourself...it's amazing where it will lead you!

CHAPTER SEVEN

STAY FRUGAL

Debt Threat

Most Americans spend 10% more than they make. That's because, while we know what our salaries are, we're less certain about how much money we're burning through in any given month. Since we live in a mostly cashless society, it's hard to keep track of how much money we debit and charge on any given day. And, believe me, some of you may really not want to know.

But that's why it's important to keep a written expense diary at least for a month or two to give you some idea of how your daily expenses add up. On *Oprah,* families in debt talked to financial experts to find out just where all their cash goes. Some parents were spending over $200 per weekend on entertainment alone, replacing quality family time with mass consumption and overstimulation. Others were racking up $100-a-day tabs on takeout food and were close to $200,000 in debt despite a good double income. Remember when a six-figure salary used to be considered more than comfortable? Nowadays, it seems most American families can blow through that in one trip through the mall!

For many Americans, debt is still a dirty secret that they don't want to face up to. Instead, as one mom on Oprah stated, they would rather maintain an image of wealth than to have to live within their means: "It's very important to look the part, no matter what the cost," she said. So imagine what she's teaching her kids! "Looking the part" will quickly take its toll on her credit, her family relationships and her children's future. And no matter what image you're going for, nothing's worth that cost.

More Money, More Problems

As many people's incomes rise, so do their expenses. Sure, part of it may have to do with burgeoning business costs…but, more likely, they start leading extravagant lifestyles that match their brand-new tax brackets. If you've ever seen *Cribs* on MTV then you'll know this happens a lot among celebrities who are riding a wave of popularity—and wiping out their bank accounts in the process. When we hear about some star going bankrupt, it's almost impossible to imagine how they managed to mismanage their money so badly. Embezzling agents aside, what could they possibly have spent it all on?

An entire town, for one thing. Actress Kim Basinger filed for bankruptcy at the height of her career after spending $20 million to buy a whole town in Georgia. Even I think that's taking real estate investing a little too far! Mike Tyson bit off more than he could chew when he wasted all of his winnings on jewelry, limousine rides, exotic rugs and a pair of tigers, burning through hundreds of millions of dollars in a shorter time than most of his fights took. Neither one of them banked on their careers taking a downward turn.

Still riding a wave of success, Mariah Carey bought a $9 million penthouse to house her 500 pairs of shoes. Kate Hudson reportedly paid $30,000 for a pair of pajamas (at that price, Owen Wilson better have been in them at the time). And Paris Hilton, who got her first credit card at 13 and has not stopped spending since, had five different parties in the world's major cities to celebrate her 21st birthday, at a cost of over $75,000 each. I realize that these celebrities are living the "if you got it, spend it" lifestyle and that, right now at least, they can afford to. But the same can't be said for the millions of young Americans who are trying to copy their style on a nine-to-five salary.

Examples like these could make up a new reality show called *Celebrity Spending Gone Wild*—only out-of-control spending isn't limited to the rich and famous. In our celebrity-obsessed culture, more and more regular people are trying to emulate celebrity style any chance they can get—even if they have to go into debt to get it. Our society has this "must-have" attitude that turns into exorbitant, irresponsible and reckless spending habits. I know of people who've gotten raises then went out and bought huge houses which they're never home to enjoy because they're busy working overtime to meet the next payment. What kind of sense does that make?

Now consider a counter example. Billionaire Warren Buffett may not be as glamorous as most celebrities, but he's a good model of someone who knew what he wanted from early on—and he happens to embody all of the steps in this book.

Buffett's fortune didn't occur overnight; it was a goal he strove toward throughout his lifetime, starting at age 11 when he worked at his father's brokerage firm. At 14, he invested $1,200 of the money he managed to save into some farmland. As a side business, he also bought a used pinball machine, fixed it up and worked out a deal to place it in a barber shop. It proved so popular and made so much side money (for him and the barber) that he was able to buy two more and put them in other barber shops in the area. A local businessman was so impressed that he bought this business from Buffett—and an entrepreneur was born!

This early lesson of investing his profits stayed with Buffet throughout his life. His real money was made when the rest of the world sold their stock in American Express due to a fraud scandal the company suffered. But Buffett took his savings and bought shares for next to nothing (about $35 a piece). Eventually, this investment grew into millions and Buffett showed all of us that you don't have to start out big to make it big.

But you also don't have to live large. Buffett is as well known for his unpretentious and frugal lifestyle as for his sharp business sense. He still lives in the same house in Omaha that he bought in 1958 for $31,500.

It's that kind of level-headed attitude that allowed him to give away billions of dollars— 85% of his entire life savings—and still have enough to live on more than comfortably. But, unlike most parents who can't say no and spoil their children (never teaching them the responsibility or reality of finances), Buffett gave that money to charity rather than to his children, who already have opportunities of their own. That's the way for the next generation to learn the value of money and good financial judgment.

Buffett giving this sum to a worthwhile charity (the Bill and Melinda Gates Foundation) was his way of investing in humanity and helping others have the kinds of career opportunities that he himself never took for granted. When he recently got remarried on his 76th birthday, the daughter of the world's second-richest man said he was "honeymooning in his office" as always. Now that's really loving your work!

A lot of essential financial strategies could be learned by Buffett's story. First, go it alone. Having a strong vision for your future is more important than having multiple partners with conflicting viewpoints. The *CEO Refresher* states that 70% of business alliances fail outright or flounder due to shifting priorities and 55% of those that remain fall apart within three years of forming. Not to mention the emotional tolls it takes on your personal relationship.

Also, let children learn about finances first-hand. Our culture of overspending (along with our increasing national debt) is being passed on to younger generations who don't have a clue about work, wise investments, economic responsibility and how they relate to all that stuff their parents give them with a simple swipe of fantastic plastic. Unfortunately, we're teaching them to play now, pay later.

Finally, growth—regarding both money and personal maturity—comes from the ability to separate the things you'd like to have from the things you have to do. Don't install a swimming pool if you're having trouble paying the monthly water bill. You'll just end up in a hole.

Splurging and Stress

Impulse buying isn't worth the temporary rush you get if it means spending the next few years worrying about a way to pay it off. I understand the temptation to want to treat yourself—after all, there is a difference between frugality and forsaking all worldly goods. But there's also a difference between buying, say, a new bag you like and buying into the brand-name obsession so prevalent in today's society.

Before charging up $2,000 for the Marc Jacobs "it" bag of the season or on an Armani anything, ask yourself if you'd be willing to spend that amount on the same product if it had an unknown label attached to it. If not, you're shelling out $2,000 for the privilege of advertising a company's logo or for a one-inch piece of fabric with a designer's name on it that's sewn into the interior lining…and that kind of stupidity is never in style. Besides the "it" bag, you're also buying a lot of extra baggage—imagine what your stress level will be for the next several years as you struggle to pay off your credit card's compounding interest.

What I don't get is this: Instead of buying designer clothes and top brand electronics you can't afford to make everyone else believe you have money in the bank, doesn't it make more sense to just put that money in the bank or invest in any of the strategies I've discussed in this book?

Extra Credit

My generation has become so obsessed with logos and stylish status symbols that we'd rather max out our credit cards than miss out on "must-have items." We're going into debt to achieve the illusion of wealth with no assets and no discernible way of getting our way out in the distant future. Young people would rather look rich and be broke than save and be smart. They pay off credit card bills with other credit cards in a never-ending cycle, which simply postpones the day of reckoning when what they owe gets so out-of-control that it winds up taking control of their lives.

Credit card use is starting at an increasingly younger age as conspicuous consumption becomes an all-consuming passion. Teenagers and twenty-somethings are ready to believe in promises of low interest rates and are all too willing to buy whatever the media is hyping this month.

Too many young people feel entitled to a luxurious lifestyle since that's what they see every day on TV or because they falsely believe that all their neighbors, who manage to buy their kids whatever they want, are doing just fine financially. But the truth is that fewer middle-class families have any substantial savings and more are going into debt trying to live up to the expectations of what it means to be middle-class. They're leasing new cars for their sons and daughters, sending maid services to college dorm rooms and spending over $1,000 a month on "upscale" campus housing so their children can get an idea of "what it's like to be an adult" (*Newsweek*). But the biggest lesson that these students learn is about how to live above their means—leading to a 104% increase in credit card debt in 18- to 24-year-olds over the last ten years.

Young people who are given everything grow up with an image that it's what they have that makes them special. Their self-worth is so wrapped up in consumerism and the lie of economic invulnerability that if their parents say they can't afford something, it has a negative impact on their self-esteem. But trust me: Not buying your 16-year-old a new car for her birthday won't cause her to suffer. Allowing her to measure love and personal value according to price tags will.

In America, it seems that the only area where the "trickle-down effect" actually works is in consumerism. The spending obsession seems to have reached all levels of society, even the very young. There was a recent profile in New York magazine in which two cousins were stopped and interviewed about their personal style. One said he loved to shop because "it's so fun. I get to pick out...my pants, like my Sean John jeans. And my sneakers. I like Jordans, and Uptowns. They're Nikes." And the older one added that he likes to wear suits because "people get to compliment you and tell you...how they like your shoes." A shoe obsession...at 6 and 7 years old! I'm still young, but I can remember back when kids talked breathlessly about "Jordan" and meant the basketball hero, not the brand name.

I was 13 when my family left our mobile home to do missionary work in Mexico and, after a year and a half there, we were about ready to come back to the States. I was already 15 years old then, but this would be the first time in seven years that I'd attend a public school. High school, no less.

By this point in my life, I had already lived in the woods, left my country and learned another language—but back in Minnesota, I really felt like an alien. The biggest concerns that my new classmates had were what kind of car their parents would buy them or what trendy clothes they should wear. Worries about when and what their next meal would be or if their parents would be out of work tomorrow never entered their minds. It was a different world from the one I was used to.

I was an outsider in my own peer group. My idea of back-to-school shopping was spending $40 at Goodwill—even though so many kids today spend more than that on one Abercrombie T-shirt with a pre-faded design that makes it look like it came from a thrift store.

It took less than a year for advertising and the desire to fit in with my friends to get to me and, before I knew it, I was your average teen spending everything I had and more on a new pair of brand-name jeans. There's something about living in a mass market society that makes this kind of behavior seem normal. It confuses our ideas about what is essential and what is extravagant.

Although I did get caught up in that materialist mentality for a little while, I soon came to realize that that was exactly the same kind of shortsighted, over-your-head spending that caused my parents' foreclosure years earlier. That's the kind of mind-set that puts one in seven young adult households earning $50,000 or less into "debt hardship." And that was exactly the kind of thing I was determined to avoid.

It's not just middle- or lower-income households that fall into this trap of overspending and have to worry about getting their way out of serious debt. As earned income goes up, impulse buying and expenses also increase, showing that even people who have a significant amount of money don't know how to spend or save it wisely—which is something that everyone has to learn for themselves.

Back in high school, I saw how easy and enticing it is to overstep your means. Yet now I know that the only way to get everything you want is not by increasing your spending—but by increasing your income.

Eliminating Emotional Debt

Is debt responsible for high divorce rates? According to a Consumers' Credit survey, 93% of couples responded that money is the major cause of stress in their marriage and over 60% fight regularly about finances. They say money can't buy love—but a lack of it can ruin your credit rating and your relationship.

Young couples learning to live together have enough difficulties without having to worry about working their way out of debt. But with lavish weddings, luxurious honeymoons and all the expenses that come with renting an apartment or purchasing that first home, a lot of newlyweds are starting out with the odds stacked against them.

We all know about the advantages of double-income families, but the other side to that equation is, except for single-occurring shared purchases like a house or furniture, there are also twice the expenses. And if the two individuals keep spending like they're still single, there's also twice the debt. Financial experts Elizabeth Warren and Amelia Warren-Tyagi have discovered that today's double-income family has less discretionary income than a single-income family did in the '70s.

Ideally, couples should have three to six months' worth of emergency cash stashed in something low-risk and liquid like a money market fund (which can be redeemed at any time, unlike a CD). Simply knowing that it's there to fall back on can reduce stress. But, in reality, most married couples have only enough savings to last them until the next paycheck, provided they aren't part of the thousands of layoffs occurring each week in America.

Too many married couples lose sight of their financial goals, focusing instead on day-to-day expenditures intended to "make their lives easier" while having the extreme opposite effect. Some families are surprised to learn that they could save as much as $9,000 a year simply by making lunch at home.

There's also the problem of the "secret spender," partners who hide purchases from their spouses in order to avoid arguments. Of course, when these splurges are discovered, there are feelings of betrayed trust and increased burdens. Eventually, overtime or second jobs are needed to meet even the minimum credit card requirements, and this can take its toll on any relationship. Want to save your marriage? Save your money.

No Pain, All Gain

Why is it so important to save? I mean, $50 at the end of the month won't change your life either way, right? Wrong.

The Consumer Credit Counseling Service illustrates how a little can add up to a lot. Take a credit card with $3,000 still outstanding and an 18% interest rate. If you met the 2% minimum monthly payment of $160, it would take eight years and a grand total of $5,780 to pay it off, almost twice your original debt.

But just by adding $50 to your minimum monthly payment, you could have the whole balance taken care of in about three years, saving yourself $1,800 in interest. President Grant never looked so good!

By now, the reasons to save should be abundantly clear. But the everyday ways to save? Still a little foggy. You've probably heard a million times how giving up the small but simple pleasures like your morning latte can make a big difference at the end of the year. But the caffeine-addicted among us know that's not the answer. While small savings on small expenses do add up, even a moderate discount on larger ticket items means a savings of thousands of dollars.

According to *Yahoo! Finance,* Americans spend a record $14.40 of every $100 in take-home pay to pay off interest on mortgage and consumer debt (that amount increases to $18.06 if you factor in other financing such as car lease payments). Right off the bat, that

means your crisp hundred-dollar bill depreci-
ates to less than $82 before you even set foot
out of the office. It's funny how we complain
about paying taxes to the American government
but we seem to have no problem handing our
hard-earned money over to American Express!

Good thing the interest on your mortgage can be a
tax deduction—unfortunately, *Moody'sEconomy.com*
shows that 2.33% of mortgages are paid
delinquently! And this is not because of job
loss or medical emergencies, but due to early
equity withdrawal used toward consumer
spending and credit card bills. How insane is it
that we withdraw money on our houses to meet
our car payments?! What experts used to refer
to as a "cycle of spending" has picked up speed
and turned into a "cyclone of spending" that
destroys everything in its path. You could lose
your home, your car, your appliances, your
plasma TV before you ever paid them off and
had the chance to actually own them!
Americans aren't only living on borrowed
money—they're living on borrowed time. Be
late on a few payments, and you won't know
what hit you.

Poor in Spirit

In today's society, we live in a culture where our possessions have actually taken possession of us. They have made us captive to credit card companies and caused us to spend over our heads with no chance of coming out ahead. Yet with all this stuff, we're still missing something.

History is going to judge us as the generation who had three television sets per household, but did nothing to relieve world poverty. The most many of us do is watch reports about it on the news in our bedrooms, kitchens and living rooms.

Today, there are companies earning more money than the economy of entire countries! Exxon Mobil, number one on the *Fortune* 500 for 2006, made $99.6 billion in revenue. Compare that to East Timor, the world's poorest country, which has a GDP of only $339 million! But with all those profits, Exxon does nothing to decrease world poverty—only to increase global pollution. (Even an episode of *The Apprentice* highlighted the importance of philanthropy in business. We tried to get celebrities to auction off something for an AIDS foundation. That was the episode I got fired on, but what a great way to be fired!)

Yes, there is a lot of money to be made in countries like the U.S. and, by all means, you should work hard to get some and get what you want out of life. But we shouldn't forget that one of the best luxuries in life is being able to help others. Charity isn't just something we give to other people; it's a gift we give ourselves.

Moving Away and Giving Back

My family survived the daily hardships of living with no heat and no running water and, by 14, I had already learned the lesson of hard work and the enormous value of a dollar. But another lesson was waiting for me down the road.

A woman, one of my mother's few friends, visited our mobile home in Wisconsin from time to time. She seemed like a nice lady but there was a certain sadness to her, even in her smile. One evening, she stayed for dinner and told us about an orphanage and schoolhouse that she went to frequently in Monterrey, Mexico. Later that night, I remember looking for Monterrey on my world map but not being able to find it.

This woman told us that the school down there needed more than just monetary help. It needed volunteers to go there and help with the classes and serve the community, which was in dire need. I could tell almost instantly that the woman's words really resonated with my parents. Maybe they saw this as a chance to help not only the orphans, but their own children, lead fuller, better lives. In any case, I knew what would happen next. I found myself in Monterrey—whether or not I could find it on my world map.

Within a short time, my family uprooted from the rich, verdant woods of Wisconsin to relocate to the dry, desert climate of Mexico. There was no translator there so I had no choice but to learn the language quickly. And I got pretty savvy about the culture in almost no time, too, especially after the local kids tricked me into eating some crazy-hot chili.

Soon, I was working alongside other volunteers and people from the community in the Bible School cafeteria, translating for newcomers and helping to teach the orphans. My own education there was invaluable, but the time I spent visiting local barrios (neighborhoods) with my family was the most rewarding.

There was a lot to get used to being transplanted to a new culture. My family moved in to a little dorm room that we shared with another family. It was a small step up from our old mobile home. Even though we had to kill cockroaches in the bathroom every morning (not the nicest way to wake up!) and our quarters were pretty cramped with little or no privacy—at least there was running water.

It seemed so funny to me when I realized that I had always thought of our lifestyle in Wisconsin as below the poverty line and I hate to say it, but I even felt sorry for myself sometimes when I wouldn't get a birthday present or Santa didn't come. But going to those Mexican barrios and seeing many families living in little huts next to a stream of sewer water broke my heart. These people would die to have the opportunity to live how I once did in America and, as we passed through border security to get back into the U.S., I could see envy on the little children's faces. These moments are forever ingrained in me and I feel that they have motivated me to use every opportunity…not to whine, not to want, but to help others because we have *so* much.

For all the hardship and initial difficulties, Mexico was an amazing experience that changed my perspective on life and taught me to value each new situation as an opportunity. After all, you could have all the wealth you've ever wanted and still not know the satisfaction that comes with enriching our world. Success isn't only measured in bank statements. Sometimes, it's measured in a child's smile.

Even though, at that time, I didn't possess much, I realized that what I did have in comparison to those children was staggering. The material goods, my health and education, my family, my opportunities, having my most basic needs met—these were all *gifts*. Just because I had them didn't mean I was any more entitled to them than any other human being; but since I was fortunate enough to have those things, I was certainly not entitled to let them go to waste.

Since no one reaches his or her goals in life without some help from someone else along the way, we in turn are obligated to help others. It's not charity; it's a responsibility and a privilege and a way of giving back. And it's not a question of what we think we can spare or how much value we place on our possessions; it's a matter of who we are as people and what value we place on human life.

Step #7: When you're in debt, what you earn isn't nearly as important as what you spend—

and what you save. The only way to get out of debt is to stop focusing on short-term wants and start thinking about what really matters to you in the long run. Want to spend more time with your family? Want to see the world? Want to retire while you still have enough energy to enjoy new adventures? Well, a new pair of $200 Nikes won't get you any closer to that. But $200 in your savings account sure will.

And, remember, some of your savings can also be used to help save others. Saving is the best route to personal wealth but giving is the best route to personal enrichment.

CONCLUSION

...Or Just the Beginning

I don't like to think of this as the conclusion. I like to look at it as just the beginning of your journey toward financial freedom.

Now that you've read my book and heard my story, I hope you realize how possible it is for you to break the cycle of insane spending and take control of your finances and the outcome of your life. It's about so much more than money. It's about understanding that everything you want and that matters to you can be yours if you're willing to work for it—and that gives you an almost unlimited amount of power over your own future.

It doesn't matter how little you were born with or how much you had to overcome. What matters is what you put into it. There are no excuses...only opportunities.

Nothing is as important as freedom—so why would you insist on indebting yourself to your company, your bank or your credit card lenders? Financial independence means that you are not beholden to others. You are not confined to a cubicle or dependent on a paycheck or limited by others' perceptions of you. You are free to achieve your own goals, decide what you want and discover your own greatness. You are only seven steps away from living your dreams of success. Push yourself forward, and in that way define your destiny.

To me, success is opening your eyes in the morning. Taking a big breath, you look at your alarm clock, making out the numbers, and realize that you have electricity. Then, looking up toward the ceiling, you stretch out your arms. You are warm and comfortable, dry and safe. And as you take your first step out of bed, it dawns on you that this day was given to you as an opportunity to serve, grow and learn. You savor that moment then immediately take *action*. You make the decision to move forward through new accomplishments, whether physical, emotional or spiritual. You have realized that each day, each minute, is valuable and no matter your situation, you search for the opportunity. Then you are truly successful.

_____

Let me share one more story with you. When I was a little girl, I used to go sit among the trees in the woods outside our farm when I felt lonely. I didn't really understand how my family and I had ended up there in Wisconsin, with no heat and no running water, and I had no idea what would happen to me next. So I would make up stories to make myself feel better and dream of all the things I wanted to be when I grew up and got away from there. An Olympic ice skater. A singer. A teacher.

Since I felt like the trees were my friends, I'd ask them their opinion about what they thought I'd be. But they'd never answer. It was then that I knew that the decision was totally up to me and I'd have to figure it out all by myself. But instead of being scared or overwhelmed by the unknown, I felt truly liberated for the first time in my life. I didn't have all the answers then, and I still don't today. But I knew I had something far more important: the opportunity, and the obligation, to make something of my life.